Democracy in the Workplace

Democracy in the Workplace

Mike Zonta

To order additional copies of this book, contact:
Xlibris Corporation
1-888-795-4274
www.Xlibris.com
Orders@Xlibris.com
37211

CONTENTS

CHAPTER ONE

Democracy in the Family

"Wouldn't it be nice if we had democracy in the family?" a teacher said to me many years ago, and I've always wondered how that might work. This treatise is an attempt to answer that question plus the larger questions it implies: if we had democracy in the family, how would that effect schools, the workplace and society in general? What would it be like to be a democratic self in a democratic society?

Or put another way, how can we ever expect to have democratic institutions in a purportedly democratic society if none of us have ever had the experience of growing up in a democratic family? By a democratic family, I do not mean a family in which everyone gets an equal vote. I think a democratic family is one in which each member of the family is free to fulfill their function without demagoguery by anyone else in the family. If I were to get Kinseyian about it, I might suggest a scale of 1 to 6 in which "1" represents a family that is run by the worst sort of demagoguery and "6" is a family which is the most democratic. Most of our families, I am sure, would fall somewhere in the middle.

It is a child's function in a family to grow up in a supportive atmosphere so that he or she can take his or her own place in society as healthy adults. It's a parent's role (whether single parent, traditional Mom and Dad or untraditional Dad and Dad or Mom and Mom) to provide a supportive atmosphere in which the child can do just that. Alice

Miller in her book, *For Your Own Good,* suggests that the following four elements be present in what I am calling a "democratic family":

1. Respect for the child.
2. Respect for his rights.
3. Tolerance for his feelings.
4. Willingness to learn from his behavior:
   a. About the nature of the individual child.
   b. About the child in the parents themselves.
   c. About the nature of emotional life, which can be observed much more clearly in the child than in the adult because the child can experience his feelings much more intensely and, optimally, more undisguisedly than an adult.

She also goes on to point out seven ways in which adults can be demagogic instead of democratic:

1. The unconscious need to pass on to others the humiliation one has undergone Oneself.
2. The need to find an outlet for repressed affect.
3. The need to possess and have at one's disposal a vital object to manipulate.
4. Self-defense: i.e., the need to idealize one's childhood and one's parents by dogmatically applying the parents' pedagogical principles to one's own children.
5. Fear of freedom.
6. Fear of the reappearance of what one has repressed, which one reencounters in one's child and must try to stamp out, having killed it in oneself earlier.
7. Revenge for the pain one has suffered.

Alice Miller is a German psychoanalyst who was raised in Germany in the 1940s. It is her contention that the reason Hitler was so successful was because he was able to reach beyond the intellect to the emotions of his followers, who, like him, were raised to obey without questions. Hitler was raised in a family that many biographers term "well-intentioned" and not untypical of its day. His father was the unquestioned head of the family and often beat Hitler and Hitler's mother. It is Ms. Miller's contention that it is not treating a child cruelly which inflicts permanent harm, but the inability of the child to respond *sanely* to such cruel treatment. At this point the pain is internalized only to become part of the psyche, that is, part of the identity of the child. Forever after (until it becomes conscious again through some sort of psychoanalysis) that painful treatment will be repeated and repeated until the child (or, as in most cases, the adult) can respond sanely to insane treatment.

Hitler went into politics. He became, in effect, his father and Germany became his unquestioning worshipers, just as Hitler's family had related to his father. Hitler was able to achieve his success not because he was an exceptional monster, but because he appealed to a lot of other "monsters" in Germany who were raised in not dissimilar circumstances. Jews became that "weak, impure" part of Hitler's own psyche which he needed to forever guard against. To call Hitler a monster lets us all off the hook. Hitler was no more of a monster than any of us. He was simply living out his undigested emotional life (as were his contemporaries living out their undigested emotional lives).

Again, Alice Miller:

> Through the agency of his unconscious repetition compulsion, Hitler actually succeeded in transferring the trauma of his family life onto the entire German nation. The introduction of the racial law has forced every citizen

to trace his or her descent back to the third generation [the exact distance back in Hitler's own lineage at which point there may have been Jewish blood] and to bear the ensuing consequences. At first, the wrong ancestry, or an uncertain one, meant disgrace and degradation; later it meant death—and this during peacetime, in a country that called itself civilized. There is no other example of such a phenomenon in all of history. The Inquisition, for example, persecuted the Jews because of their religion, but they were offered the chance to survive if they accepted baptism. In the Third Reich, however, neither behavior nor merit nor achievement were of any avail; on the basis of descent alone a Jew was condemned, first to be demeaned and later to die. Is this not a twofold reflection of Hitler's fate?

1. It was impossible for Hitler's father, in spite of all his efforts, successes, and advances in career from shoemaker to chief customs inspector, to remove the "stain" in his past, just as it was later forbidden the Jews to remove the stigma or the yellow star they were forced to wear. The stain remained and oppressed Alois [Hitler's father] all his life.

2. At the same time, the racial laws represented the repetition of the drama of Hitler's own childhood. In the same way that the Jew now had no chance to escape, the child Adolf at one time could not escape his father's blows, which were caused, not by the child's behavior, but by the father's unresolved problems, such as his resistance to mourning over his own childhood. It is fathers such as this who are likely to drag their sleeping child out of bed if they

cannot come to terms with a mood (perhaps having just felt insignificant and insecure on some social occasion) and beat the child in order to restore their narcissistic equilibrium.

The Jews fulfilled the same function in the Third Reich—which attempted to recover from the disgrace of the Weimer Republic at their expense—as this sleeping child.

One final quote from Alice Miller shows just how important and far-reaching are the consequences of child abuse:

Both child abuse and its consequences are so well integrated into our lives that we are scarcely struck by their absurdity. Adolescent's 'heroic willingness' to fight one another in wars and (just as life is beginning!) to die for someone else's cause may be a result of the fact that during puberty the warded-off hatred from early childhood becomes reintensified. Adolescents can divert this hatred from their parents if they are given a clear-cut enemy whom they are permitted to hate freely and with impunity. This may be why so many young painters and writers volunteered for the front in World War I. The hope of freeing themselves from the constraints imposed by their family enabled them to take pleasure in marching to the music of a military band. One of heroin's roles is to replace this function, with the difference that in the case of drugs the destructive rage is directed against one's own body and self.

This certainly addresses two major world problems today—drug addiction and violence. With the world's nuclear arsenals tending to limit another major world war, where is all this stored up adolescent "heroic willingness" going to go? Gangs? Self-indulgence? Suicide? Alice Miller's suggestion (and mine) for a solution is, perhaps not surprisingly, psychotherapy of some sort or another. This is, to my understanding, the only way to make the unconscious conscious and thereby free ourselves from our childhood bonds. If we don't free ourselves from our unconscious motivations, then we will simply continue to enact them, finding an abusive father at work or a controlling mother as a wife. To the degree that we are not healed from our undemocratic families, we will carry our early training with us wherever we go and find again undemocratic schools, workplaces, etc. Those of us lucky enough to have lived in a fairly democratic family or those of us who have unlearned our undemocratic early training will help transform the school, the workplace and society. (Although I must say that I think those who have to "unlearn" their undemocratic upbringing will probably appreciate their new found health a lot more than those to whom it came with little or no effort)

Alice Miller doesn't think there is any pedagogy for child "rearing" which is not poisonous. It is not the pedagogy which raises a child. It is the individual people who are his or her parents. We, as children, detect, consciously or unconsciously, who our parents are and what their *real* values are. Robert Coles explains in his book *The Moral Intelligence of Children:*

> A baby has learned to love, even as it has been loved, to
> reward with effort those who have exerted effort on its behalf,
> to accept and please those who have accepted it, have been so
> pleased by it. This reciprocity of feeling and behavior, this clear

connectedness, as it broadens and enlarges all concerned, is an early expression of a shared respect, a mutuality of regard, a moral mutuality, a capacity of the baby no less than its parents (and other adults who appear from out of nowhere, it seems) to see the world through the eyes of others, to be grateful, to link arms in what becomes, really, a shared effort, parents doing their best, the baby doing its best. All of the above takes place so gradually and pleasurably and un-self-consciously, with no abstract articulation of sentiment, no conceptual chatter (the "naturalness" of those early months and years) that one is apt to forget how much self-absorption is forsaken by most babies, in favor of an embrace of others, their hopes and their expectations; their *values* [Coles' italics]. The baby becomes a willing student who keeps its eyes quite literally on the teacher, senses what is wanted, offers it—joins a small community and earns its membership in it: a good citizen carrying his or her fair share of a family's weight.

Indeed, children, it seems, are eager to become good citizens of their families. This is extended to the desire to be good citizens in kindergarten and elementary school—except for those children who have been injured by nature (such as diseases of autism or mental retardation) or nurture (in instances in which the dysfunctionality of the parents is so profound that it obviously reflects on the child's ability to function "democratically" in the early school years). And much of the learning involved at that age is how to play *fair,* that is, democratically. This can be very difficult, if not impossible, coming from a family system which is more demagogic than democratic. But, as is illustrated by the following example from Robert Coles, sometimes the mind has ingenious ways of reconciling seemingly irreconcilable influences. But at what cost to the child?

A young boy who had taken to heart a family's split moral imperatives as they got lived day by day had developed a split, an aching heart. A teacher had told his mother: 'When he gets rebellious, you can see his eyes filling up.' The parents had trouble figuring out that particular 'symptom,' as they called it. I appreciated their obliging gesture towards psychopathology, but I thought to myself at the time, and with Tim's help would come to know, that this issue was not only clinical but, again, deeply moral: how to reconcile different, even contrasting or opposing values that are both spoken and enacted by one's parents. The solution: to be defiant, peremptory, though with tears of regret and sadness, sullen words, a contentiously waving hand, modified by expressively knowing, mournful eyes, eager to undo what has been said or done.

By the time adolescence comes along, most children have a solid sense of their family's place on the democratic/demagogic scale of 1 to 6. And, as Alice Miller suggests, adolescence is the time for heroic action (if the child is from a more democratic family) or *reaction* (if the child is from a more demagogic family). But still, morality plays a key role as Anna Freud indicates:[1]

Over and over I'm told that a child is terribly 'difficult,' extremely 'rebellious.' I ask for details, and get plenty of them—and as I listen I begin to understand the parents' sense of what is going on, but I have to admit (and I do, to them!) that I hear something else, commonly; I hear a demanding conscience at work [in the adolescent], with the rebelliousness

---

[1]   Quoted in Robert Coles' *The Moral Intelligence of Children*, p. 147.

a reaction to it. This can come as a surprise to the parents who have been pronouncing their own children virtually lawless, without moral standards, at the mercy of their every whim and fancy!

In my own experience as a substitute teacher in a very isolated and poor region of Oakland, about 2/3rds of the children in the six classes I taught (grades 6-8) were difficult and rebellious children. I lasted one day of a 30 day assignment not only because of the "difficult" and "rebellious" children but because there was no expectation from the school or from anyone else that these children could accomplish anything. There were no lesson plans, not much of an idea really of what to do with these kids for 40 minutes besides entertaining them with movies or trying to get them to read the really boring and mostly irrelevant reading materials.

Gerald Heard in his *Five Ages of Man* sets up a very interesting idea about the stages of childhood and how they relate to the stages of man's development from caveman to civilized man. Heard divides the stages of mankind into five which correspond to the stages of any particular person: 1) Infancy relates to pre-individualized man as the pre-individualized baby with its symbiotic relationship with its mother relates to primitive man and his pre-critical, pre-self-conscious mind—the 440,000 years or so of hunter-gatherers also referred to as traditional (and sometimes matriarchal) society. 2) Childhood relates to the time in the history of humanity which Heard calls the "Heroic Age" and also that time in a child's life in which he or she seeks to assert her or his own personality. Starting about 10,000 B.C., Heroic man sought to overcome the "superstitions" of magic (the casting of spells and communication with the nonhuman and unseen) and the urge for tactile closeness which had the effect of mesmerizing and thus de-individuating. Children, too, seek to understand and demystify their world. To be a hero demands rigorous rules of life which are probably best exemplified in Western literature in the *Iliad* and the *Odyssey* and in Indian literature in the *Bhagavad-Gita*. These are stories of what it means to be a hero with the qualities of courage, endurance and curiosity being at the forefront. According to Heard, "The hero's ways: violence instead of craft, blows rather than words, of a father's unbrooked authority, a woman's subservience, and a son's submission: these, the only right ways, must be the only possible ways for a man who is worthy to live." Obviously, the Heroic age was the beginning of what we now call the Patriarchy. Children in their "terrible two's" exemplify the beginning of this heroic effort. 3) The third stage of development of a human and of humanity is what Heard calls the Ascetic Stage. This is the stage of adolescence for a human being and begins around the 8th century B.C. for most of "developed" humanity (meaning India, China and the Mediterranean). The Ascetic Age was a response to the Heroic Age in which men (and women) instead of seeking to stand out from the crowd as an individuated self sought to be lost in society, nameless and therefore safe from the excesses of the individual and subsumed into a uniform mentality which uses propaganda and denial as its source of power. The Roman Catholic Church epitomizes this effort as did its Inquisition. In China and India, the importation of Buddhism supplied their ascetic needs as Christianity supplied the ascetic needs of the Mediterranean. In teenagers, belonging to the "in-crowd" or to a gang or to the chess club all fulfill a similar purpose of providing a safe haven from the excesses of the Heroic age of childhood. 4) Starting around the 15th century, the Ascetic Age was replaced by what Heard calls the Humanic Age. This is referred to in individual humans as the first maturity. In Western civilization, it is called the Age of Enlightenment, the Renaissance. It is the beginning of the Age of Duality. Science and the scientific method are looked on as "saviors" from the excesses of the Ascetic Age and the power of religion and the Church just as every age is a response to the excesses of the previous age. This relates to both human history in general and each of our individual personal histories.

Heard again:

> The Heroic Age had served the purpose of destroying the primal magic . . . . The new Man of the Renaissance, the man of recently intensified self-consciousness, aware of his distinctive and separative individualism, was keen to reason and sharply equipped to argue . . . . The hero wished to be outstandingly famous and so feared to be shamed. The ascetic feared being expelled and hoped to be forgiven his guilt. The total individual now saw not merely no reason why he should prefer the pricking of his own finger to the death of any of his fellows who were of no use to him, but no reason why he should feel either shame or guilt.

Heard says this age lasted from the mid-15th century to the beginning of the 20th century. Through Humanic man's super-rationality, he cut himself off from any intuition or emotionality. Humanic man lasted only a relative short time and eventually had to admit the impossibility of its task—reaching happiness through reason. (The rise and fall of the Third Reich may have been Humanic man's swan song.) The Humanic age spawned four revolutions in the West: the revolution of Protestantism and the beginning of the disintegration of the Church; the political revolutions against monarchism; the economic revolution called the industrial revolution; and, finally, the psychological revolution popularized by Freud's "discovery" of the unconscious. Eventually, though, Humanic man had to admit that he/she and life (or nature) were not separate, but inextricably united.

H.G. Wells, who was perhaps the chief promoter of progress through science also recognized the limits of scientism. In an essay called *The Scepticism of the Instrument,* he asked the question, "How do we know that we can apprehend an objective world?" At the turn of the 20th century, physicists such as Max Planck and Niels Bohr began to realize that the search for absolute objectivity which had been the scientific paradigm for 2400 years had come to an end and had been replaced by what is now called field theory and the theory of relativity. In the biological sciences, the concept of "mutation" was added to the simple Darwinian theory of the "survival of the fittest." Thus, in a species, a sudden, unexplained, unpredictable change could occur at random (just as electrons behave unpredictably). Ecology, the first branch of science to seek to understand the interdependence of organisms and their environment, began at this time.

The final stage of humanity's development and of an individual human's development Heard calls the second maturity or "Leptoid Man." With the understanding of ecology that all life is interdependent, humans unlike any other animal have evolved without the outer shells of insects and without even the hair (for the most part) of other animals. Humanity's greatest attribute is its nakedness and vulnerability. It is through this increased sensitivity to his or her environment that humans can evolve the most rapidly. And this is why our children take such a long time to mature—so that they will have a longer time to learn. (Buckminster Fuller says that all other animals are designed for specialized tasks. Only mankind was meant to be a generalist.[2]) Leptoid man, according to

---

2   Fuller, Buckminster, *Operating Manual for Spaceship Earth*, p. 13.

Heard is what is required for the postmodern world. Leptoid man will be able to evolve in consciousness through vulnerability. But like the errant electrons, it will require an unpredictable leap into the unknown by a critical mass of people for this new stage of humanity to be completely born. Most of us are stuck at first maturity, according to Heard. The second maturity in most individual humans and in humanity as a whole is still in its embryonic stage.

I include Heard's theory because it has given me a greater respect for the tasks which children are required to at least attempt—nothing short of the recapitulation of the history of humanity from caveman and its symbiotic relationship with the world (represented by the baby's symbiotic relationship with its mother) to Heroic man and its efforts to break free of the stultifying superstitions and depersonalization of the past (as represented by the child's brave efforts to seek out on its own for the first time away from mother) to Ascetic man and his effort to seek solace and anonymity in groups (just as the teenager seeks safety in his or her clique) to first maturity of humanity during the Renaissance (and when an adolescent comes of age and begins a family or a career) to the age in which we presently live—the second maturity of humanity which is the beginning of a whole new paradigm of humanity as universal citizen (which is represented by the individual universal citizen). According to Heard's theory, each person repeats the history of humanity in his or her life time in this manner, just as each fetus repeats the history of cellular life on this planet from the single celled amoebae to the fish-stage fetus with gills, to the monkey-stage with a tail to the almost human baby.

Ontogeny repeats phylogeny. That is, each person's individual history repeats the history of the race after having gone through the rather remarkable conception process in which the fetus repeats the entire history of life itself on this planet. Heard even sees this process as predictive in nature. He feels that since most children are born with relatively large heads, that this represents the next level of humanity as a whole—a level in which our "heads" are a lot more developed than they are now.

In a democratic family, a child's role is very important indeed as are the roles of his or her parents.

CHAPTER TWO

The Oedipal Conflict

One of the jobs a child has in a healthy family is making the successful transition from baby to child, from child to adolescent and from adolescent to first maturity, to use Heard's terms. (Second maturity comes later, if at all.) Unsuccessful completion of any of these transitions will cause life-long arrested development. Part of the successful transition from baby to child is resolving the Oedipal conflict. If the Oedipal conflict is not resolved by the time adolescence comes along, the child will not have the necessary ego strength to handle the challenges of adolescence. If it is still not resolved by the time the adolescent is expected to enter into first maturity, then the adolescent will be doubly hampered in adulthood by not having resolved the issues of childhood or adolescence.

The Oedipal complex was a term derived by Freud which was based on the myth of Oedipus who *unknowingly* killed his father and married his mother. While not all psychoanalysts agree about the importance of even the validity of the Oedipal complex, Freud was not the first to come up with the idea that the Oedipus myth represents a paradigm for humanity. Aristotle canonizes *Oedipus* in his *Poetics* and, of course, Sophocles wrote his Oedipus trilogy based on the Oedipus myth in 400 B.C. or so.

In the myth of Oedipus, Laius consulted the Delphic Oracle because of his (Laius') prolonged childlessness. The Oracle said he should consider his childlessness a blessing because whoever was born to his wife Jocasta would end up killing him. He thereupon banished Jocasta who managed nonetheless to get him drunk, and nine months later a son was born to her. Laius in his anger had the boy's feet pierced with a nail and tied together, and he left him hanging on a mountain. A shepherd found the boy and named him Oedipus which means "swollen feet" due to his feet being deformed by the nail wound. Oedipus was brought to the city of Corinth. One day a Corinthian youth taunted Oedipus because he did not in the least resemble his parents. Oedipus went to the Oracle who immediately cried, "Away from the shrine, wretch! You will kill your father and marry your mother!" Since he loved the couple who he thought were his parents, he left Corinth straightaway. At a crossroads, he unknowingly ran into his biological father, Laius, who was in a chariot while Oedipus was on foot. Laius gruffly told Oedipus to make way for his betters. Oedipus said he had no betters except God and his parents. Laius ran over Oedipus' foot with his chariot (another swelling no doubt occurred). Oedipus killed Laius' charioteer with his spear and had Laius dragged to his death by whipping his horses to a frenzy.

Laius had been on his way to the Oracle to ask how he could get rid of the Sphinx who had been harassing every wayfarer by asking the same question and, when they couldn't answer it correctly, the Sphinx killed them on the spot. Later, when Oedipus arrived in front of the Sphinx, the Sphinx asked the same question as always: "What being, with only one voice, has sometimes two feet, sometimes three, sometimes four and is weakest when it has the most?" Oedipus answered, "Man, who crawls on all fours as a baby, has two feel as an adult and sometimes walks with a cane as an old person." Hearing this, the Sphinx leaped off a mountain and killed herself. The people of Thebes were so grateful to Oedipus that they made him king, whereupon he married Jocasta, the newly widowed queen.

When a plague hit Thebes, Oedipus again went to the Oracle. The Oracle said, "Expel the murderer of Laius!" Not knowing she was referring to himself, Oedipus sentenced Lauis' murderer to exile. Another seer, blind Teiresias, finally told Jocasta that it was Oedipus who killed his father and married her. After seeing confirming letters from Oedipus' adopted parents, Jocasta hung herself and Oedipus blinded himself with a two-pronged broach which belonged to Jocasta. Oedipus was exiled from Thebes and wandered for many years guided only by his faithful daughter, Antigone.

This story brings to my mind the Old Testament stories of Joseph, of Moses, and of Ruth and the New Testament story of Christ. Oedipus' name, "swollen foot" because of the nail which pierced it at the beginning of the story is certainly reminiscent of the nail which pierced Christ's feet and hands near the end of his story. But, like Joseph in the Genesis story, perhaps Oedipus had a "swollen" sense of his own importance. Like Joseph's sense of being the apple of his father's eye, Oedipus claims "I have no betters except God and my parents!" Like Moses, he wanders in the desert and like Ruth in the story of Ruth and Naomi, Antigone never leaves his side.[3]

In the story of Joseph, Joseph is sold into slavery by his brothers and eventually ends up as a prisoner of Pharaoh. When Joseph interprets the Pharaoh's dreams, he is then given command over all of Egypt. When Oedipus is able to answer the Sphinx's question, he is made the king of Thebes. But he still has to deal with his as yet unconscious past. He still doesn't know that he killed his father and married his mother. A plague descended upon Thebes as a plague was to descend upon Joseph's Egypt. Joseph interprets the Pharaoh's dream of seven fat calves and seven lean

---

3   Ruth saying to Naomi: "[W]hither thou goest, I will go. Where thou lodgest, I will lodge. Thy people shall be my people and thy God my God." Ruth 1:16. The Bible, King James version.

calves to mean that there would be seven years of plenty and seven years of famine, so the Egyptians were able to store up and survive the famine and Joseph was put in charge of the entire operation. Among those who came to him for food during the seven lean years were his brothers who had left him for dead. He had to charge them and then discharge them: "I am Joseph, your brother, whom ye sold into Egypt. Now therefore be not grieved, nor angry with yourselves, that ye sold me hither: for God did send me before you to preserve life.[4] Joseph grew by his ordeal and realizes that it was not his brothers who sold him into slavery, but it was the working of a higher intelligence, if you will, trying to have its way with Joseph. Now, Oedipus has to deal with his past, too. He is confronted with it suddenly and he reacts violently. His mother hangs herself and Oedipus blinds himself with his mother's broach. Oedipus can no longer look at his children or at his world. And yet in blindness, he is no longer blind to his past. Knowing his past, he can no longer bear to look at the present.

Oedipus is a tragic myth. If only Oedipus had Joseph's insight, that it was not anybody's fault that he did what he did, but that it was for the greater education of all humanity. We all go through our own Oedipal complex, but we don't have to gouge out our eyes when we realize what our desires are, not do we have to kill ourselves. Oedipus went to his tragic end so that we don't have to. Much like Christ did. The Oedipus myth has appealed to us throughout Western history because there is truth in it. But it is left up to Antigone, Oedipus' daughter, to die a heroic death, a death based on principle. The moral of the story is that we can all live a life of principle once we have transcended our own Oedipal complexes.

---

[4]   Genesis 45: 4-5

*   *   *

The Oedipal complex applies to both girls and boys. Although it is sometimes referred to as the Electra complex in girls, most authorities simply use the term "Oedipal" for both sexes. And, according to Freud, the Oedipal complex is both positive and negative in little boys and little girls. In his work *The Ego Gild the Id,* Freud says:

> . . . that is to say, a boy has not merely an ambivalent attitude towards his father and an affectionate object-choice towards his mother, but at the same time he also behaves like a girl and displays an affectionate feminine attitude to his father and a corresponding jealousy and hostility towards his mother.

> [The complete Oedipus complex is a series] with the normal positive Oedipus complex at one end and the inverted negative one at the other, while its intermediate members exhibit the complete form with one or other of its two components preponderating. At the dissolution of the Oedipus complex the four trends of which it consists will group themselves in such a way as to produce a father-identification and a mother-identification. The father-identification will preserve the object relation to the mother which belonged to the positive complex and will at the same time replace the object-relation to the father which belong to the inverted complex: and the same will be true . . . of the mother identification. The relative intensity of the two identifications in any individual will reflect the preponderance in him of one or other of the two sexual dispositions.

If the preponderance of a boy's sexual disposition is toward mother-identification and father objectification, the boy identifies with his mother and wishes to be loved genitally by his father. This is not merely a "passive aim" as defined by Freud but a homosexual object choice. A little girl who wants to be loved genitally by her father would also be making a "passive aim" but it would be a heterosexual object choice. If a little girl wanted a more "active" aim, she would identify with her father and objectify her mother. This, also, would be a homosexual (lesbian) object choice.

The castration fear arises in either the passive Oedipal or active Oedipal complex of a boy. In the active Oedipal complex, a boy is afraid of castration by his father because he is hoping to usurp his father's role and is afraid of his father's vengeance. In the passive Oedipal complex, the fear of castration is caused by the realization that in order to be genitally loved by his father the boy must have the genitalia of a female and thus he fears losing his penis.

Penis envy is the female correspondent to male castration anxiety in the primary Oedipal conflict, according to Johanna Krout Tabin. She writes in *On the Way to Self: Ego and Early Oedipal Development* that there is not only the classical Oedipal conflict in most children from about the age of 4 to 5-1/2 but there is also the primary Oedipal conflict at about age two. In the primary Oedipal conflict a boy may have castration anxiety due to his fear that his mother wants to get close to him and he would therefore lose his boyness which in graphic terms is represented by his penis. A girl, on the other hand, might have penis envy due to an overpowering mother. In order to be closer to her father (and away from the mother), she might want to be like him, i.e., to have a penis.

Girls who have a "positive" Oedipal complex and mother-identify and father objectify have a lot in common with boys who have an "inverted" Oedipal complex and do the same. Likewise, boys who have a "positive"

Oedipal complex and father-identify and mother objectify have a lot in common with girls who have an "inverted" Oedipal complex. The only difference being their gender and thus their equipment. "Positive" Oedipal girls and "inverted" Oedipal girls might both suffer from penis envy: the "positive" as a way to be closer to her father (if she had a penis) and the "inverted" so she could penetrate her mother like her father. "Positive" Oedipal boys and "inverted" Oedipal boys might both suffer from castration anxiety: the "positive" as an expression of fear of retaliation from the father for being attracted to the mother and the "inverted" might suffer castration anxiety since his penis could be seen as being superfluous in making genital love to the father.

I had an "inverted" Oedipal complex. That is, I identified with my mother and objectified my father. I remember being very upset with my mother for "coming on to me" by calling me her "handsome little man." I loved feeling "beautiful," but, I think, was hoping that it would be my father instead of my mother who "wanted" me (although I could barely admit that even to myself). One of my favorite fantasies as a child was feeling very handsome and irresistible and being in bed with my mother *and* rebuffing her. But this is where the conflict came in. I needed my mother for emotional and physical support but I also wanted to be independent of her. So, not unlike many "positive" Oedipal girls, I played along because I saw no alternative. I sublimated my sexuality (my desire for my father) in order not to upset my mother.

In my story, I was not able to resolve this Oedipal situation naturally, that is, with a strong enough ego to be able to realize that I could be sexual with my "father" (or, in other words, with men in general) without "killing" my mother. When I was 8 years old, my mother died a sudden and violent death. In fact, she was shot dead in front of me and my brother by one of her female friends who was also a member of our local church. Instead of feeling horror, I felt relief and then, of course,

shame. Finally, my mother was out of my way. I had my father to myself.
I didn't have to resolve my Oedipal conflict. "Destiny" resolved it for
me. Shortly thereafter, I remember asking my father not to remarry. That
way I could keep him to myself. A year or so later, when he did decide to
get remarried, I remember feeling tremendous relief. No longer would
I have to feel the shame of what I felt (or was supposed to have felt) at
my mother's death.

The interesting part of this whole story is that it didn't end there at
8 years old or at 10 years old. A pattern had begun which was to replay
itself out over the next 40 years. I discovered the pattern in October of
1996, about 15 months after I had begun my then-present job. I had
just gotten my B.A. degree and 1 wanted to quit my job. I was able to
convince myself that I needed to stay but only after rigorous argument.
I knew when I started this job that I wanted to beat my old record—15
months. Then I realized that it was more than a record—it was a pattern.
I had not been able to last at a job for more than 15 months or so in my
whole life before feeling I had to quit. Even when 1 went to college from
1964 to 1965, I only lasted 15 months. Then I joined the Navy which I
had to leave under duress after 15-16 months of a two-year hitch. (I told
them I was willing to commit suicide to get out, which was true.) And in
no job since then have I been able to work more than 15-16 months. At
one job which lasted nearly four years, 1 was able to stay there, but only
by quitting twice and being rehired twice.

The pattern was discovered first. Then I went back and found the
original "mold" which was, I believe, those 15-16 months that I had
my father to myself. My mother was killed in August 1954. My father
remarried in March 1956. That's a period of 19 months, but with an
extra 3 or 4 months of getting ready for the wedding, that fits the pattern
perfectly. Having been the original "mold" of how long I was able to keep
my father all to myself, that pattern was to be repeated unconsciously

throughout the rest of my life until I uncovered it. But not only did this affect my work life, it also affected my love life. Whenever I got close to a man that I was really attracted to, I would sabotage myself and wouldn't allow myself to be with him because I didn't want to feel how selfish I was again—not to be sorry at my mother's death but only happy to have my father to myself!

I think this is what is meant by the Oedipal conflict. It's not an easy conflict for any child to resolve and they can only resolve it through a strong enough ego identification which comes with age and proper family support. (In a recent news release from the Society for Research on Child Development, no significant difference existed using the standard psychological assessments of children raised by heterosexual parents and lesbian couples.) If these conflicts are not resolved as children, they can be resolved in later life but only by conscious effort. I thought I had to have one or the other—my mother or my father (and most kids think so, too). I chose my father, but didn't *really* want to have my mother killed. Most kids do feel they have to make this choice, and it can be an ego-killer. Or it can be resolved with time and the natural growth process in a loving home and the realization that the urgency of the Oedipal choice is not all that urgent after all.

Just why is this Oedipal or Electra complex necessary and when is it triggered? As Joanna Krout Tabin indicates, the primary Oedipal relationship usually occurs around age 2 when the child is met with many identity problems. While the first years of life are spent usually in some sort of symbiosis with the mother by both girls and boys, the boy's challenge at age 2 is to begin to separate himself from the mother with the concomitant fear of the loss of protection/love. The second source of conflict in boys in a "normal" primary Oedipal relationship is his realization that his sexual feelings for his mother bring him into direct conflict with his father. Of course, the obverse is true of an "inverted" primary Oedipal relationship—the boy becomes aware that his desire for his father places him in direct conflict with his mother and his primary source of emotional and physical support. The third source of conflict for a "normal" two-year-old boy is his realization that the person that he is trying to separate from—his mother—is also the person who he is yearning to get closer to. In the case of the "inverted" two-year-old boy, the problem is that the person he is seeking to get closer to sexually, his father, probably would not be available for him in any way emotionally and may be quite put off by what might be considered "inappropriate" interest on the part of his son. The happy resolution of all of these conflicts is a healthy two-year-old with a beginning sense of ego formation based on the integration of a chosen gender identity from role modeling based on either or even on *both* parents and a healthy (i.e., safe) sense of separation from his mother.

A two-year-old girl's ego formation is also begun with the same three challenges only in a somewhat different way. First is her increasing need for a sense of a separate identity. The second problem a two-year-old girl faces is that the person that she is seeking to separate from—her mother—is the same sex as she is and is thus her gender role model. Thirdly, a "normal" two-year-old girl is beginning to become aware of sexual feelings for her father which brings her into direct conflict with her mother, or, in the "inverted" case, the two-year-old girl is beginning to become aware of sexual feelings for her mother—and thus she has the same problem that the young "normal" boy has of being sexually attracted to the person who she is trying to separate from. Also, as in the case of the "inverted" boy, the "inverted" girl may suffer (but probably not to the same extent) a sense of denial due to the perceived "inappropriateness" of her feelings. In a young girl, "inversion" could lead to "penis envy" since some sort of penis would be needed (unconsciously) to fulfill (unconsciously) her sexual desires just as a young boy might feel "castration anxiety" if he felt sexual desires for his mother, knowing that he is in direct competition with his father. The happy resolution is a girl with a healthy ego formation based on a chosen gender identity based on role modeling from either or both parents and a healthy/safe sense of separation from her mother.

Quoting from Joanna Tabin:

> . . . [S]uicide in the male occurs four to six times as frequently as in the female (Shneidman 1976) . . . . We have seen that for the boy the issue of separation/individuation is tied to fears of engulfment. We recall that at the two-year-old stage the child does not possess a sense of time beyond the here and now. Because of this and the categorical mode of thought the child employs, the toddler sees in relation to existence only the possibilities of omnipresence and total nonexistence. Thus the little boy responds to an immediate threat of engulfment with either wishes to disappear or for mother to disappear; in either case, disappearance meaning annihilation. This extreme a response is prompted because engulfment itself means an end to his ego, and thus his end to his existence.

> A girl's very existence is not similarly endangered in the parallel situation. Fusion with mother reinforces her gender identity; and while fusion does impinge upon her autonomy and sexuality (and such issues can give rise to intense, guilt-related behaviors), they do not carry the same emotional urgency as the question of existence.

Unsuccessful resolution of the primary Oedipal conflict may cause very serious problems in later life for men as well as women. Men who cannot resolve their Oedipal conflicts may become sadists toward women—thus fighting in the only way they know how the overpowering feeling of engulfment by women by taking control of them preemptively. Or a man who cannot resolve his fear of being overpowered by a woman could simply become a Don Juan—charming and seductive on the surface but fearful of any relationship deeper than that. Or such a man could become suicidal such as the Japanese artist, Yukio Mishima, who committed suicide. Although suicide is within the cultural milieu of a samurai swordsman, his earlier life indicated that Mishima was still a very Oedipal child (emotionally) at the time of his death. Theodora Abel in the *Journal of the American Academy of Psychoanalysis* (1978) writes that "[a]fter his death Shizu, his mother, is reported to have said, 'My lover has returned to me.'" Mishima became a samurai swordsman, Ms. Abel speculates, because he needed the most masculine identity possible to overcome his lack of a well-integrated ego identification.

In most native societies, it is the boy, not the girl who has to undergo initiation rites. Perhaps these societies know instinctively that boys need special help in getting through this crisis in human development. Usually they are taken away from the women and are surrounded by men who are the only ones who can help them become independent of their mothers. Even in our own culture, little boys are encouraged to be adventurous and daring probably more so than little girls not in any sense of sexism, but simply because it is more vital psychologically for the boy (and for an "inverted" girl) to break away from his (or her) mother than for a girl (or an "inverted" boy) to do the same thing. (Cultural sexism comes in later when people assume that what was psychologically valid for a child is necessarily valid for the adult as well.) The mother is usually, after all, the girl's role model and so separation is not expected in the girl child. Although if a separation is not made, usually it is the young girl's sexuality which has to be sacrificed. A little girl cannot be both "fused" with her mother and have sexual feelings for her father. That would place her in competition with her mother and thus risk the girl's psychological safety.

In sum, a boy's (or an "inverted" girl's) psychological makeup demands him to be risky and daring by striking out and becoming an independent self. The alternative is engulfment *as* a woman. (An "inverted" girl could probably "pass" for a while role modeling herself after her mother. According to this theory, lesbians have more psychological leisure to "come out" than gay men.) A "normal" girl, on the other hand, doesn't have to worry about engulfment since her gender identity is not threatened by staying "fused" with her mother, but her sexuality *is* threatened. (An "inverted" boy also has to worry about "engulfment" to a degree but can probably get by more easily than a "positive" Oedipal boy since mother is also his gender role model.) So if she doesn't want to become an "old maid," a "positive" girl will need to gradually and safely liberate her sexuality. Thus the initiation rites in native societies and the early socialization of each sex has its beginnings in psychological requirements.

An unresolved Oedipal conflict can cause sadism, Don Juanism, splitting (seeing women as Madonna or whore, for example) and suicide in "positive" men *and* "inverted" women. In "positive" women *and* "inverted" men, an unresolved Oedipal conflict can cause spinsterism or it can cause splitting which in these cases means being able to be *either* strong and independent but with a limited sexual identity (identifying with a strong mother and not wanting to be in competition with her for the father) *or* being a very sexual woman (or gay man) but being unable to get along in the world (needing a man to make her *or* him complete). It is theorized that just as sadism is by far more prominent in men (and lesbians?) than women due to unresolved Oedipal conflicts, so is anorexia far more common in women who fear becoming independent of mother. The two year old girl, still concerned orally (anal issues come soon thereafter) represses her sexuality so as not to jeopardize her security with mother (the source of most food). She becomes "mama's little girl." When adolescence comes along, the girl can no longer hide her sexuality, but she has not developed enough of an ego identification to allow herself sexual autonomy and so she tries in the only way she knows how to break free from mother/food—denying mother by denying food. At the same time that she is denying food, she is thereby making herself skinnier and skinnier and therefore less physically feminine and less of a threat to mother as well. This vicious cycle can only be resolved by resolving the Oedipal conflict.

Interestingly, gay men (that is, "inverted" boys) who also suffer from unresolved Oedipal conflicts probably follow the same pattern as unresolved "positive" girls—that is, denying their sexuality and becoming "mama's boys." When adolescence comes along for most gay boys (which may be in their 20's or 30's), however, instead of continuing to try to repress their sexuality and thereby not offend or compete with mother, it seems many gay boys go in the other direction and risk offending mother (damn the guilt!). But if the Oedipal conflict is still unresolved in these adolescent gay boys, then the guilt, the shame, the fear is still there. So not only do gay adolescent boys have to deal with the shame with which society regards them, they also have to deal with their own internalized shame and guilt and unconscious fear of no longer being "mama's little boy." This is undoubtedly a very strong contributory factor to the physical symptoms known as AIDS just as anorexia is the physical result of deep unresolved psychological problems mostly in girls.

During the primary Oedipal conflict at age two, the child has no sense of a past, only the immediate present. Something is either good or bad—there is no gradation. They are beginning to become aware of anal abilities as opposed to just oral abilities. Emotions are intense, there is no sense of future and they are prelinguistic for the most part. During the classic Oedipal conflict at age five, the child has a greater sense of himself or herself as having a past and a future and that it will someday become an adult. The child is beginning to be able to think using words. Resolution of the primary Oedipal conflict results in a child who has a greater sense of himself or herself and his or her place in the family. Resolution of the classical Oedipal conflict results in a boy or girl having a greater sense of himself or herself in society. By the time adolescence comes along, any unresolved conflicts will begin making their mark in our lives and we either settle into a pattern of slight to severe neurosis or we get help!

Though each of us chooses a path from which to begin our journey in life—either we identify with mother and objectify father or we identify with father and objectify mother—still that is only the beginning. To maintain our childhood identities throughout the rest of our life (based on our parents' identities) would be to truly lead a limited life. Even if we are fortunate enough to have resolved our Oedipal conflicts and march into adulthood hale and hearty, we still have to give birth to a spiritual self which is innate in all of us and even pre-human—Heard's "second maturity," Emerson's "oversoul," Richard Bucke's "cosmic consciousness." This self which the mystics have written about for ages cannot be limited to male or female for it is both at the same time. It is androgynous just as the universe is androgynous. Both gay men and women may have an advantage here since both have already been forced to explore the territory of androgyny in depth.

I think we do choose our own Oedipal components—whether we want to be "positive" or "inverted"—but I don't think it's a conscious choice. It is, as Freud suggested, simply a matter of trying on various attitudes and seeing which one fits us best.

All of this is very important to democracy in the family, the workplace and society because if we are not emotionally and spiritually ready to participate with our whole selves at work or in society, then we need to get some help. Blaming our lousy childhood is not going to make our present lives any better. In fact, many people who *seem* to be fighting for justice or equality or the underdog are really trying to resolve their own unresolved childhoods and thus their cause, whatever it might be, is undermined from the outset and will never be achieved until personal resolution takes place. If someone is espousing feminism but they're really using that profound and evolutionary movement as a cover for their own unresolved Oedipal complexes, charges of "patriarchy" may actually be an expression of unresolved rage at Dad. Likewise for the proponents of multiculturalism. If they are projecting onto mainstream society (i.e., "the Man") their own unresolved childhood feelings of impotence and Oedipal rage, they will be undermining their own cause from the outset.

It's easy to scorn theories like "penis envy," but it's just a term. It doesn't have to be taken literally. What it stands for is a stage of development. "A girl who feels that little boys have a better time in life, and who admires the masculine role may either try to emulate males, or may, by reaction, despise them."[5] On the other hand, of course, Karen Horney points out that a little boy goes through a similar stage when he becomes aware that only a woman can give birth. Melanie Klein in *The Psycho-Analysis of Children* and *Envy and Gratitude* explains

---

[5]   Pincus, *Secrets in the Family*

how both boys and girls have feelings of jealousy about their mother's breasts which when unresolved in the "positive" Oedipal male (and the "inverted" Oedipal female) is shown by the mixture of admiration and derogation of the breast. Calling them boobs, tits, honkers, headlights, etc., shows an unresolved castration anxiety (to use Freud's term). And how many male businessmen or males of any sort (other than gay males) have advanced beyond such mixed emotions towards a woman's breasts?

The dysfunctions of our families create the dysfunctions of society and vice versa, unto the seventh (and more) generation.

CHAPTER THREE

Dysfunctional Families

"Happy families are all alike; every unhappy family is unhappy in its own way," is Tolstoy's first line in *Anna Karenina*. The University of West Florida supplies the following do-it-yourself survey online[6] to see if you come from a dysfunctional family:

DYSFUNCTIONAL FAMILY TRAITS

Answer the following questions according to whether you strongly agree (2), agree somewhat (1), or don't know/disagree (0).

1. Particular individuals in my childhood home were treated as though they mattered much more than others (as opposed to everyone being treated equally valuable). 2 1 0
2. The emotions of some individuals in my childhood home were considered much more important than the emotions of the others in the home. 2 1 0
3. One parent was consistently trying to fix the other. 2 1 0
4. Our family had many secrets we kept from others. 2 1 0
5. Each person in our home had specific roles we had to play and roles we were not allowed to play. 2 1 0

---

[6] Their internet address is uwf.edu.

6. Guilt and shame were used a great deal to control behavior in my childhood home. 2 1 0

7. One parent was either physically or emotionally not there for me very much in my childhood home. 2 1 0

8. There was much hidden anger in my childhood home. 2 1 0

9. During my childhood, I felt my physical and emotional needs were not met very well. 2 1 0

10. As a child I remember feeling empty quite often. 2 1 0

According to the UWF:

> Very few people score near zero on this questionnaire because very few people come from perfect homes.

> - High score 15+ indicates that you might have come from a very dysfunctional home and should seriously consider guidance for dealing with the issues involved.

> - Very low score may mean that you are in massive denial about your childhood and need help in accepting your issue."

I scored from 14 to 19 taking it at different times.

I have been consciously "working on myself' since at least 1969, but when I first heard John Bradshaw on PBS use the term "dysfunctional family" in the late 1980s, I felt a profound sense of relief that at last somebody was talking about me and my family in a way that I could quickly and easily grasp. It was dysfunctional. I came from a dysfunctional family. I don't know if Tolstoy's line is true or just clever and I sincerely wonder if there is anything like a functional family. But still it was nice to hear someone give a name to what so many of us experienced in our families.

Whatever dysfunctions there are in a family probably involve one or more of the three great mysteries of family life: birth, copulation and death. All families have their own myths or secrets which define how they relate to these great themes of life. "Secrets may be private to one family-member; or tacitly shared with others; or unconsciously subscribed to by all family-members, often from generation to generation, until they become a myth" according to Lily Pincus and Christopher Dare in *Secrets in the Family*. The authors go on to state that there are two kinds of secrets: those which involve actual events which are kept secret from other members of the family and those which have no basis in fact but which are unexpressed fantasies usually involving jealousy, rivalry, love and hate.

One of the premises in this thesis is that the work place for many of us, whether we like it not, has become a second family. If you are a television fan, you will probably remember Mary Richard's famous last lines from the final episode of TV's "The Mary Tyler Moore Show" in which she says that she tries to convince herself that the people she works with are just the people she works with instead of her family. The scene closes with a semi-comic group hug which nobody really wants to break, even as they walk out of the room. Mary Richards was a fictional single working woman, but for many of us, whether we have our own family or not, our co-workers are our family or at least our second family. (It would be interesting for each workplace family to take the dysfunctional family test above and see what happens. I'm sure that most workplace families would be in as much need of a good family counselor if not more than a traditional family.) And as each family has its secrets and myths so does each workplace have its own secrets and myths and, like the family, the workplace myths center around the subjects of birth (new hires), copulation (who's "doing" who) and death (who's getting fired or quitting or being kicked upstairs).

Years ago, when I brought up the subject of workplace family myths at my own place of work, we came up with some of the following myths about our workplace:

1. We don't have enough money.
2. The support staff is uninterested or unable or unwilling to do anything more than secretarial tasks.
3. We are always on the verge of downsizing.
4. The best way to solve a problem with a co-worker is to take them out to lunch.
5. Support staff is always interested in free food, no matter how stale.

My family (from age 10 on) was a Brady Bunch type of family consisting of my father and me and my brother from one family and my step-mother and two step-sisters from another family. These were some of the family secrets we held:

1. Our previous families were never discussed.
2. My mother was never shot and killed.
3. My father was a saint (and so was my step-mother).
4. We were a happy family.
5. At the center of our happy family was a happy and successful marriage.

*   *   *

In the family the parents are the only ones who are allowed to have sex. But surely this sexual activity or lack thereof affects the rest of the family. In a family in which the parents have a healthy sex life and are not still working out their own Oedipal conflicts,[7] the excitement and pleasure their parents get out of each other is bound to stimulate their children's own sensual and sexual longings, and it is bound to stimulate sexual fantasies of an incestuous nature. In fact, if there are not some incestuous feelings between mother and son, for example, or father and daughter, then the child will probably grow up thinking there is no way anyone of the opposite sex could ever find them attractive. This, of course, brings up the subject of same sex attraction. It is no wonder that most gay men have such a hard time adjusting to adulthood. With a father who in most cases wants to keep whatever sense of incestuous attraction he may have for his son completely bottled up, there is not much chance of a gay boy growing up into a healthy gay man without undergoing a lot of unnecessary grief. Mothers are usually more free to admire the beauty of their daughters even if it does verge on an incestuous feeling, and therefore lesbians usually are a lot more stable than gay men.

In an unhealthy family, that is, in a family in which the marriage is unhealthy, children are especially vulnerable. "The central factor to which the children respond seems to be the parents' unrecognized shared fantasies, especially their fantasies about sexuality. For the pubertal and pre-adolescent child who has to find his own identity and come to terms with his own sexual fantasies, the parents' shared confusion or anxiety about sex presents a threat for which the child is trying to get help by developing attention-seeking symptoms."[8]

---

[7]   I am using the term "Oedipal conflict" as a general term here for unresolved childhood trauma.

[8]   Pincus, *Secrets in the Family.*

In the family, it is the parents who have most of the decision-making power and the family is based around their sexually-based relationship. What about our workplace "parents"? Well, they certainly have most of the power and most of the money. So let's say power and money replace sex at work as the matrix of the work family. The further you go up on the hierarchy of work, the more money you make and the more power you exert. So, at work, as in the family, hope is held out that one can "grow up" and become an adult. In the family "growing up" means beginning your own sexual relationship and starting your own family. At work, being a "grown up" means becoming a manager or becoming a boss which imply that non-managerial workers are, in effect, "children".

This dichotomy (the dichotomy between children and adults) is rife throughout our society. In the military, we have officers and enlisted. In industry, we have management and workers. In education, we have teachers and students. In real estate, we have owners and renters. These dichotomies are all based on our original dichotomy of the family. To have a democratic family would go a long way towards lessening this dichotomy in the rest of society. But to have a society of adults would go even further. If we really had a society of adults—fully functioning "first maturity" adults—then this dichotomy of management/worker, officer/enlisted, teacher/student, even owner/renter, would be much more fluid than it is today. It is the fear of familiarity breeding contempt that keeps this dichotomy going. It is the fear that the "children" (workers, enlisted, students, renters) will discover that the "adults" (management, officers, teachers, landlords) are really no different than they are—people at different levels of development as human beings.

An example of the dichotomy of workers can be found in two books about spirituality at the workplace. Both The *Heart Aroused* and *Parcival's Briefcase* speak of overcoming emotional and spiritual problems at work, but in both these well-intentioned books, the readers are assumed to be management. No mention was ever made of the emotional or spiritual problems which support staff (secretaries, word processors, receptionists, janitors) might encounter. It was assumed that if you were intelligent enough to be reading these books that you must be in some kind of managerial or supervisory position.

An example of the dichotomy between enlisted and officer is the case of the late Chief of Naval Operations Mike Boorda who rose up from the ranks to become CNO and then in May of 1996 killed himself over a minor scandal about wearing medals which he may not have been eligible to wear. He was the first enlisted man who crossed over to become an officer and eventually the Chief of Naval Operations. He came from a dysfunctional family. His father was an alcoholic. The Navy was a refuge for him. He even lied at the age of 17 saying he was 18 so he could get into the Navy. The enlisted men loved him, but if he had come from the officer class instead of the enlisted, it probably would have been easier on him to deal with the pressure. He felt a very strong connection to his sailors, even writing them a separate suicide note (along with one to his wife and family). The military culture applauds hierarchical leadership. Perhaps Boorda never got over his humble roots. We all are inner children even though we appear as adults. And here is the root of our society's dichotomy.[9]

In *The Heart Aroused,* David Whyte admits that, "We walk through the door into the organization every morning looking like full-grown adults, but many parts of us are still playing emotional catch-up. The griefs and traumas of childhood follow us around, asking for attention . . . . The rest of the psyche may grow and mature, closing like a protective callus around the wound, but the wound itself remains isolated . . . . We look around at work and see outwardly self-possessed adults, but know

---

[9]   Information about Boorda comes from Time Magazine, May 27, 1996 issue.

from long experience that the layer of composure and control can be very thin. A professional environment seems especially conducive to the appearance of the wounded child. All the components of control and pleasing are present in good measure, ready to trigger the emotional allergic reactions that do everything but bring us out in a rash." But Whyte also sees that "[t]he psychological view of this situation would be to say that we are projecting our fears onto parental figures, particularly those at work whom we feel have power over us, and must overcome this tendency. But the soul's view might be to see these traumas as constantly repeated opportunities for courageous articulation, opportunities that the soul takes endless pains to engineer and place in our way until we step back through the doors of perception, back in to the life promised to us before we sealed ourselves outside."

Every family begins with a marriage. The marriage is the focal point of a family. "The first principle that seems of great importance to us is that the motivations that take people into marriage, sustain its perpetuation and give it its particular qualities, are largely unconscious . . . . It seems to be obvious that the reasons for the suddenness and intensity of falling in love are usually unconscious. The choice of a marriage partner seems often to have been made very quickly, on the basis of relatively little conscious knowledge, and with, as it turns out, great accuracy of complementarity and fit of personalities and even life experience of the partners."[10] R.D. Laing says in *Self and Others*: "Each partner strives to find in the other, or induces the other to become, the very embodiment of the other whose co-operation is required as a complement of the particular identity he feels compelled to sustain." The relationship can be one of growth and flowering of the self through using the other as a conscious projection of oneself and thus working on oneself through

---

[10]   Pincus, *Secrets in the Family*.

the other, or the relationship can become violent and rigid and deadly through not recognizing the other as a projection of one's own hopes, wishes and longings. If one partner projects onto the other his own repressed feelings of violence or anger, the other partner will no doubt express those feelings for him which may lead to a resentment on the part of the first partner instead of a resolution of the repressed feelings which was one of the original unconscious reasons the two got together in the first place. Sometimes the "well" partner projects her or his illness onto her or his partner who becomes the "ill" partner and in this usually unconscious agreement both partners thereby share the "illness" between the two of them. Sometimes couples marry not to project onto each other but to reinforce their images of themselves by marrying someone as much like them as possible.

The complementary emotions and desires which begin a marriage are usually based on earlier infantile and childhood relationships. If our infantile and childhood needs were poorly met, we will probably repeat the pattern until we resolve it through therapy of some sort. A woman whose childhood was damaged by an alcoholic father might marry someone who turns out to have a drinking problem. Or a boy who had unresponsive parents may find difficulty in finding responsive partners or will find a partner who seems to more than make up for an unresponsive parent. The interesting thing to me about all this is that the unconscious is always trying to get it right even if it has to try it over and over again. This indicates to me that underneath all the unresolved emotional needs of each of us lies a profound intuition that fulfillment of needs is natural and that it is not natural to go through life with unmet emotional needs. That's a very hopeful sign for family life and for work life.

According to Lily Pincus and Christopher Dare, ". . . the pattern of relationships most commonly called to our minds in our work with families, couples and individuals, seems to derive from the time when the little child can realize something of the intensity of his own longings towards his parents whilst at the same time recognizing that the parents are themselves a couple with a particular and potentially intense relationship with each other from which the child is excluded. This is of course the situation already described as the Oedipus complex. The way this group of experiences is patterned and evolves will crucially affect subsequent fantasies evoked by sexual longings for love affairs and marriage."[11]

At the foundation of a marriage, of course, is a wedding. Here is the wedding ritual described by Pincus and Dare: "The wedding ritual in our culture underlines the fact that the daughter never belongs to herself; she belongs either to the father who gives her away or to the husband to whom he gives her. It seems astonishing that there is no part in the ceremony for the bridegroom's father or for either mother. For the father this ritual can involve considerable strain which is sometimes physically demonstrated in illness, heart attacks or even death, following soon after a daughter's wedding, in which the father has not only to let his daughter leave home but also to renounce his own unconscious incestuous fantasies and longings."[12]

Why is there family abuse? According to Richard Gelles in *Unhappy Families,* "People abuse family members because they can. There are rewards to be gained from being abusive: the immediate reward of getting someone to stop doing something; of inflicting pain on someone as revenge; of controlling behavior; or of having power." Mr. Gelles is speaking of family violence which, of course, is strictly forbidden at work, so abuse in the work family has to go underground (or be repressed until one gets home). Mr. Gelles also notes that "[t]he police are known to

---

[11]   Pincus, *Secrets in the Family.*

[12]   Ibid.

respond faster when people are beating up a stranger than when they are beating up a family member" and "[c]riminals and assassins account for only half of all homicides; the other half, our family members, destroy one another with handguns they have purchased to protect themselves from strangers."

David Gil writes in the same book *(Unhappy Families)* that violence is whatever gets in the way of a person's natural development. It could be physical violence or emotional violence as one might find in a dysfunctional family or institutional and societal violence as one might find in schools, hospitals or bureaucracies of any sort or in the underclass ghettos of society. Although these types of violence—institutional and personal—are different from each other, they feed off of each other. There would be no individual violence if there was no institutional violence and vice versa. Gil's view is that "prevention of family violence requires a revolution in our way of life that would rearrange or redesign our modes of production and distribution in a manner that is conducive to the full development of every child and adult and aging person." What we do now, he says, is allow fewer and fewer people to control more and more resources (natural and monetary and even educational) and thereby require more and more people to work under the direction of fewer and fewer, thus denying most people the opportunity to work at their own initiative and rate of development. "Nobody gets hired," Gil says "unless, directly or indirectly, he or she makes possible the further accumulation of resources for those who control the workplace. Work processes are designed not to enrich the life of the workers, but to enrich materially the ones who employ the workers. Work gets divided into meaningless fragments because some experts have figured out that it is more profitable if it is meaningless. About 90% of the work force will spend their work life in meaningless, repetitive routine activities under the control and direction and design not of themselves but of others. That is the typical situation of everyday work life."

This Gil terms as violence. Gil views capitalism (whether American capitalism or state-run capitalist societies like the former Soviet Union) as inherently violent because they use people as factors of production to meet economic needs regardless of the person's biological or psychological (not to mention spiritual) needs. The success of capitalism requires enough workers who are willing to work for low wages and thus create a profit. This requires a surplus of workers which is why unemployment is necessary for a successful capitalistic society. With unemployment as a necessity, there is competition at every level of society for a "piece of the pie," and competition breeds violence, and violence breeds dysfunctional families, and dysfunctional families breed more dysfunctional families.

Gil concludes: "Short range, the first policy step is eliminating the illusion that unemployment is normal or necessary for a healthy economy. Then, full self-employment which means to transfer the resources with which people work to the control of the people who do the work: self-direction, or, to use a very ancient term, democracy in the workplace. (The funny thing is that we tend to talk about our way of life as a democracy. A democracy means a way of life that is run by people. Ours is run by those who control the people's resources and not by the people.) I think we have to aim for full participation in work by all, under control by all working people in their work places. We then have to ensure that the product of work be shared in accordance with the needs of all members of communities in relation to their age, health, and so forth. Work should not be compensated at fixed rates in hierarchical terms. The reward system, whether it operates in kind or through money, ought to be geared to the needs of people and not to what positions people have succeeded to obtain, and it ought to take care of everybody. These are policies which would gradually reduce the experience of violence in everyday life and would thus reduce and eventually eliminate interpersonal violence . . . . To me, a search for alternative modes of social organization is the only way to overcome violence in the family."

Gil thinks the only answer lies in changing society. I think we can approach the problem from both angles by changing both the individual and society, but it will probably take second maturity men and women to do it.

CHAPTER FOUR

Democracy in the Workplace

Five hundred years ago, capitalism was a progressive step up from the feudalism and mercantilism of the day. Today, capitalism is at its greatest height having practically vanquished communism everywhere in the world, including China. But, as Thomas Kuhn states in his *Structure of a Revolution,* when a paradigm reaches its peak of inevitability is one of the signs that a new paradigm is about to emerge.

Perhaps the new economic paradigm is democracy. But democracy requires autonomous people, that is, people who can stand on their own two feet. Earl Shorris says in *The Oppressed Middle: Politics of Middle Management, Scenes from Corporate Life* that "[t]o dare to answer the call of autonomy a man must prepare himself by learning to love reason. Then he will be thrilled by justice and even the smallest instance of the rule of law will set him trembling with emotion. The recognition of dignity in the priceless equality of men will bring him the kind of joy he expected only from the birth of a perfect child. He will think of freedom as an exultation, for he will know that it is the only heaven men can make."

Speaking about egalitarianism, Shorris says: "A manager who knows that his subordinates are his equals becomes the equal of his superiors. If he does not teach his subordinates to fear him, he may not learn to fear his superiors. If he respects their lives, he may learn to respect his own. If he permits them dissent, he may arrogate dissent to himself."

In *The Reenchantment of the World,* Morris Berman gives us a chart of how the new paradigm (Heard's second maturity) might compare with the old Cartesian (scientific method) paradigm. This is a part of that chart:

World view of modern science	New Paradigm world view
Nature is known from the outside, and phenomena are examined in abstraction from their context (the experiment).	Nature is revealed in our relations with it, and phenomena can be known only in context (participant observation).
Goal is conscious, empirical control over nature.	Unconscious mind is primary; goal is wisdom, beauty, grace.
Mind is separate from body, subject is separate from object.	Mind/body, subject/object, are each two aspects of the same process.

An evolutionary paradigm must happen, however, of its own accord. It cannot be forced on society as Lenin and others tried to do earlier this century.

As late as 1800, according to Paul K. Conkin in *Freedom in America,* 90% of American white men were self-employed and today less than 10% are self-employed. In the 18th century, free enterprise meant being free to be your own boss. He says: "Americans boasted of a new political order that made possible a nation of property owning freemen. Here there would be no special privilege, no large monopolistic estates based on laws of descent, and slavery excepted, no large class of people excluded from ownership of the means of production. There would be no trading companies, basking in special government charters or franchises. At least all white males, despite a wide range of ability and varied levels of attained wealth, would be of one social class—the proprietary. Each man would eventually be able to own his own farm, shop, or ship. He would thus be free and independent, in control of his own life, under no lord or boss."

With the industrial revolution, things changed. The factory became, in effect, substitute parents in large part because many of its workers were children. As late as 1900, 18% of all factory workers were under 18 years of age. "Mills like Boston Manufacturing Company, in Waltham, Massachusetts, the Merrimack Cotton Mills, and Lowell Corporation brought in farm girls and housed them in dormitories, with housekeepers to watch over them, to make sure they were in by 10:00 p.m. and that their moral lives weren't compromised."[13]

After World War II, there were a million men enrolled in college on the GI bill. These men started to join corporations. And the "organization man" with the gray, flannel suit was born. "Writer after writer," says Amanda Bennett in *The Death of the Organization Man,* "in the late 1950s and early 1960s chronicled the trend as the post Depression fear and anxiety gradually melted into that need to be part of a group, a crowd, a gang. And for many, the corporation became that gang . . . . From the hereditary position of corporate management, which lasted from the 1850s to well past the First World War, middle management became a job for Everyman."

"Plastics!" whispered Mr. McGuire to Benjamin Braddock in Mike Nichol's 1967 film *The Graduate.* And so a new generation of post-organization men was born in the 1960s. The *new* organization "men" were, first of all, also women. This changed the dynamics of the workplace once again from the exclusive "old boy's club" to a new sort of experiment in equality between the sexes which, of course, is still ongoing. The women's movement as well as the downsizing in the two last decades, especially at the middle management level, has eroded employee loyalty. Entrepreneurship has increased (especially among women) as have company perks such as employee-owned stock options,

---

[13]   Bennett, Amanda, *The Death of the Organization Man*

and, in the more progressive companies such as software companies, the gray flannel suit has been replaced by T-shirts and jeans and campus-like settings in which informality is the rule and recreational activities are provided for relief from around the clock coding.

Today Americans seek fulfillment not in proprietary independence (i.e., owning their own land and resources) but in consumption. "Perhaps this stage [America's beginning and the westward expansion] ended in America before it had to," says Paul K. Conkin in *Freedom in America,* "and in part because American proprietors placed their greatest emphasis not upon the primary moral meaning of property—the universal right of all people to have access to nature—but upon a secondary and morally distorting meaning—the right to retain what one had acquired, however large and however much it foreshortened opportunity for others."

In America's early years, government—colonial, state and federal—transferred land and natural resources to private individuals and corporations to ensure rapid private development but with few conditions—"no requirement of need, no rules for responsible use, no limits on amount owned, no public retention of the social increment."[14] This cozy relationship between business and government lasted until the panic of 1837 when states defaulted on bond issues and left public works uncompleted and state-supported banks were allowed to fail. In the 1840s, when business began to recover, it had little use for government anymore and thus began the idea that "economic freedom" meant as little interference from government as possible, although business kept up its close relationship with politicians whenever they needed laws which would help their businesses.

Until 1842, state courts ruled that unions were a "common law conspiracy in restraint of trade"[15] and even after 1842 union activities

---

[14]   Cochran, Thomas C., *Freedom in America.*

[15]   Ibid.

were strictly relegated. The United States Congress did not question *caveat emptor* ("let the buyer beware") until the food and drug acts of 1906 and 1907. Private enterprise has until recently been thought none of society's business and thus truly a private exchange between a buyer and a seller. Finally, gradually, and even suddenly, the American citizens have realized that an economy based solely on private profit and regardless of the benefits or costs to society is not a sustainable economy. "This, then," says Barry Commoner in *Freedom in America,* "is the reason for the mounting list of regulations, for the growing bureaucracy, for the erosions of freedom that have followed in the wake of our determination to improve the environment. There is, deeply embedded in the design of our systems of production and economics, a basic fault that is the common cause of both the degradation of the environment and the erosion of our freedom. The fault, I believe, is that we are governed in what we produce, and how we produce it, by the aim of maximizing private profit rather than social value. We can resolve this fault by creating a production system that judges the value of its products by their use and not by their profit, and an economic system that is committed to serving social needs . . . and thereby sustain[ing] the personal freedom which is the historic foundation of American democracy."

This country was founded on the belief, as Jefferson says, that government governs best which governs least. But this is only a negative view of freedom—meaning freedom from something. Freedom must not only mean freedom *from* excessive government, but freedom *to* create one's own future. This freedom must be used for the good of the individual in society, not isolated from it. J.B.S Haldane wrote, "The Greeks had a word for the man who used his freedom to turn his back on society. The word was . . . in English, 'idiot.'"

We can no longer afford an economy of continued growth. We need to start thinking in terms of continued improvement. To create such an economy will require a new kind of politics, one no longer based on compromise but one based on consensus, taking into consideration what is best for the entire country, rather than just a particular area or industry. Freedom from feudalism was very frightening to the feudal lords and to the emerging capitalists. Both were uncertain of their futures. Likewise, freedom from capitalism will be equally frightening to both capitalists and to value-based entrepreneurs.

Ultimately, the solution to capitalism is individualism (evolution of the individual self). Each stage of history has a corresponding characteristic. From the Renaissance on, fame has seemed a natural desire of most people. This was not true of Medieval citizens. In the middle ages, everyone knew who they were—you were either a peasant or a lord. In the Renaissance, this was not the case and so fame became a desirable antidote to the uncertainty of increased individualism.

The emergence of capitalism came about because of the increased individualism of society. It began in Italy more so than Western or Central Europe because Italy was a more important center of trade and thus exposure to different cultures. There was also the trouble which Machiavelli alluded to: Italy's many independent centers of power. Out of this rose a moneyed class which helped destroy the feudal structure of Italy and bring about "urban masses of exploited and politically suppressed workers."[16] Although they no longer had the protection of a safe place to belong, people had a greater sense of themselves as individuals. With this new sense of individualism, they started to explore the world.

But capitalism had its greatest flowering not in Renaissance Italy but in the Central and Western Europe of Luther and Calvin. While Renaissance Italy was inspired mostly by a group of moneyed elite,

---

[16] Fromm, Eric, *Escape from Freedom*, p. 45.

it was the urban middle class of Central and Western Europe which responded to Luther's and Calvin's religious individualism. A new sense of time emerged as well. Time was beginning to mean money and work was seen as a value in itself. Begging orders in the church were seen as unproductive and thus immoral. The clocks of Nuremberg have been tolling on the quarter hour since the 16th century.[17] With the beginning of capitalism came the beginnings of competition which was not really a factor in the Middle Ages in which everyone had his or her place and there was no career ladder to climb. Commerce now was valued above any artistic or scientific pursuit. Capital began to rule society. One assessed one's value by how much money he or she had whereas in the Middle Ages one assessed one's value by one's inherent position in society.

Luther and Calvin both gave the individual tremendous spiritual freedom and power which translated later into economic and political freedoms. The dark side of Protestantism is its belief that man is inherently evil and only by negating one's individualism could one do the will of God. Calvin added the doctrine of predestination so that you were either eternally damned or eternally saved before you were born—and you didn't know which. This added the element of a kind of irrational activity to life and to work. Work was no longer just to provide the necessities of life. Work became a value in itself, not because of what it produced. Workers became their own internal masters who were much harder on themselves than any external master could ever hope to be. These workers began to amass capital not to spend it, but because they were not sure whether they were predestined for eternal damnation or not, and they might as well get in all the self-negation they could before they found out.

---

[17]   Ibid, p. 58.

This, of course, created an underlying hostility and resentment in society, one which largely went unexpressed, but which was there nonetheless. Luther and Calvin personally represented this type of repressed hostility which appealed to so many in Central and Western Europe in the 16th century. Calvin's idea of an arbitrary God, who without any particular reason prejudges people to a life of eternal damnation or heavenly bliss, is the product of a man with a lot of repressed hostility. By teaching people that the only way to gain God's graces was by humbling themselves through unceasing efforts, hard work, thrift and by purifying yourself in order to become "God's instrument," Protestants became the middle class engine which propelled capitalism into the world-changing paradigm it has been. It also created a mentality which led the world to fascism in the mid-20th century and to the mass consumerism and anti-individualism of today.

"The word 'employer' contains the whole story," says Eric Fromm in *Escape from Freedom*. "[T]he owner of capital employs another human being as he 'employs' a machine. They both use each other for the pursuit of their economic interest; their relationship is one in which both are means to an end . . . . It is not a relationship of two human beings who have any interest in the other outside of this mutual usefulness." And this relationship permeates all of society. One's worth is defined by how much value others place on him or her. Thus one's self-confidence or self-worth is not usually internally created, but externally created which is the reason why "fame and fortune" are so all important in this society—because "fame and fortune" will bring self-esteem, or so it is presumed.

In a society which values economic success over everything else, individualized services as might be found in smaller businesses in which a seller might actually personally know his or her customers would be and have been increasingly marketed out. Large chain stores which have little or no contact with individual customers are overtaking "Mom and Pop" stores just because they are more economically feasible. Money is more powerful than humanity at the beginning of the 21st century.

The cynicism of modern advertising campaigns shows us this. Advertising shows us that conformity is more important than individuation. Advertising shows us the "normal" conforming person having fun doing "normal" things with whatever product they are selling. Acceptability is what is being sold, and the product is only a by-product, so to speak. Those who do not wish to submit to society's dictates of what is normal are considered neurotic and those who do submit to society's dictates truly are neurotic.

According to Eric Fromm,[18] there are two types of neurotics—sadists and masochists. Both help a person overcome the inevitable feelings of powerlessness and aloneness one faces in a capitalist society. Fromm suggests calling the sadism/masochism syndrome a symbiosis which results in the negation of the individual self into a symbiotic state with some other individual or entity. In the 1930s and 1940s, sadists had a heyday in Nazi Germany and fascist Italy and Japan. One of the ideological fathers of Nazism, Moeller van der Bruck, wrote: "The conservative believes rather in catastrophe, in the powerlessness of man to avoid it, in its necessity, and in the terrible disappointment of the seduced optimist."[19]

Then there are the destructive types. They do not wish to control or submit to society or parts of it as the sadists and masochists do, they wish to destroy it and at least temporarily rid themselves of the terrible aloneness in their lives. Destructiveness seems to be a part of societies which repress its members either spiritually, politically, economically or

---

[18] Ibid, p. 158.
[19] Moeller van der Bruck, *Das Dritte Reich*, pp. 223, 224.

any other way. Fromm suggests that the amount of destructiveness in a society is equal to the amount of expansiveness curtailed.[20]

Conformity seems to be on the ascendancy today. Conformity is the tendency to go along with the "normal" as represented by the not-so-silent majority. Alex de Toqueville referred to this as a peculiarly American trait—the tyranny of democracy. Eric Fromm puts it this way: "In the course of modern history the authority of the Church has been replaced by that of the State, that of the State by that of conscience, and in our era, the latter has been replaced by the anonymous authority of common sense and public opinion as instruments of conformity . . . . We have become automatons who live under the illusion of being self-willing individuals . . . . The right to express our thoughts . . . means something only if we are able to have thoughts of our own."[21]

To have thoughts of our own means we have to know who we are. To find out who we are, we have to *be* who we are. Who we are is not an intellectual conclusion. It is a spontaneous reality. And it can only be done socially, that is, within a group. Oscar Wilde points out in *The Soul of Man Under Socialism* that "Know thyself" "was the credo of the Old World and "Be thyself"" will be the credo of the New World. To be yourself requires spontaneity and spontaneity can only result from a psychology of joy, not from a psychology of dysfunction (like Freud's) or a psychology of suffering (like Christianity). The new psychology, according to Wilde, will be a psychology of joy.

We are only one step away from feudalism today. In order to change our present paradigm, we need to agree on three things: we need to agree that people are not basically evil or lazy and that we *are* inherently good; we need to agree on the equality of all people, not on the basis of

---

[20]   Fromm, Eric, *Escape from Freedom*, p. 183.

[21]   Ibid, pp. 241, 253.

anything other than our existence; and we need to agree that all people have a right to the "good life," whatever that means to each person.

It will be through work (and at work) that this new society will be achieved. It is through work (and at work) that each of us will achieve our individuation. Not work as enslavement or work as the competitive grasping for material things or even work for our families, but work which fulfills and transcends the aloneness inherent in freedom and evolving individuality. Through our work we can connect ourselves again with nature by being natural, by fulfilling *our* nature. An atmosphere of joy in what we do will create the atmosphere for others to find their own spontaneity as well. And when we as a society reach critical mass, we will have achieved a new millennium.

CHAPTER FIVE

Democracy in Society

Oscar Wilde saw voluntary socialism as the answer to the problems of capitalism. In his essay *The Soul of Man Under Socialism,* he said: "Yes; there are suggestive things in Individualism [Wilde equates individualism and socialism.] Socialism annihilates family life, for instance. With the abolition of private property, marriage in its present form must disappear. This is part of the programme. Individualism accepts this and makes it fine. It converts the abolition of legal restraint into a form of freedom that will help the full development of personality, and make the love of man and woman more wonderful, more beautiful and more ennobling. Jesus knew this. He rejected the claims of family life, although they existed in His day and community in a very marked form. 'Who is my mother? Who are my brothers?' He said, when He was told that they wished to speak to Him. When one of His followers asked leave to go and bury his father, 'Let the dead bury the dead,' was His terrible answer." Eric Fromm called the family the "psychological agent of society."[22] And even more frightening, I think, is that each of us, to the degree we are still beholden to it, are also the agents of society.

Buckminster Fuller in his landmark book "Spaceship Earth" and David G. Gil in his 1979 book "Beyond the Jungle" point out that the problems involved in supplying material security for every person on

---

[22] Ibid, p. 287.

Earth are not mainly material or scientific any more but rather are cultural and political. Gil sees human societies composed roughly of two types (of which none are completely one type or the other). The first is the nature-loving society in which everyone shares in the work to be done and in the fruits harvested. The second type of society is the pseudo-individualistic society in which everyone is out for his or her own self or immediate family believing that resources are scarce and that we must compete with each other in a "survival of the fittest" mentality and in which charity or welfare is provided for those most unfit. I use the term pseudo-individualistic because an authentic individual would not allow himself or herself to be a part of such a self-destructive vicious cycle. Real individuals in our world today are transcendent of society but are at the same time requisite for community.

Capitalism made men forget who they were (serf, prince, land lord, peasant or *villein*—interestingly, the etymological root of our present word "villain") and become more interested in what they owned. But you can't own anything unless you are deeply involved with it. In essence, you can only own what you love. Capitalists are too busy making money to be deeply involved with any of the possessions money can buy. So capitalists end up loving money for its own sake, having forgotten why they so desperately wanted it in the first place. Individuals or proto individuals (being the first of a kind) are deeply involved in life. Life is what they love. Life is their workplace.

David Gil says: "The principle of social inequality is known to result in conflict and competition; control, domination, and exploitation; alienation and deprivation, obstructions to human development and waste of human and material resources. Hence it tends to reduce individual liberty for everyone, though privileged individuals may not perceive the progressive deterioration of their own liberties. The principle of social equality on the other hand . . . should result in social harmony and cooperation; freedom from control, domination, and exploitation by others; free development of individual capacities and conservation of human and material resources. It would, admittedly, eliminate the freedom acquired by a minority in inegalitarian societies to control, dominate, and exploit others for selfish ends and privileges, and it may therefore be perceived as a severe constraint on their liberties."

Gil goes on to say: "Free access to and egalitarian use of resources should therefore be implemented in a decentralized manner, through democratic, horizontal coordination and cooperation among self-directing, equally entitled, relatively small yet economically viable communities of producers and consumers . . . . Unnecessary, unproductive, and wasteful work such as advertising, banking, insurance, real estate deals, military enterprises, etc. would be eliminated, so that only work necessary for human well-being and enjoyment of life would be carried out."[23]

The competitive workplace affects not only our lives at work, Gil argues, but everywhere. Road rage is one example of how the competitive society is getting out of hand. According to Mizell & Co. of Maryland, the "majority of aggressive drivers are relatively young, relatively poorly educated males who have criminal records, histories of violence, and drug or alcohol problems. But hundreds of aggressive drivers—motorists who have snapped and committed incredible violence—are successful men and women with no known histories of crime, violence, or alcohol and drug abuse." According to California Highway Patrol Officer Phil Jones, "My personal analysis is that it's all about space. All day long, we're at work, and unless we're the CEO or the mayor, we're told what to do all the time. At home, it's the same thing—wives, husbands, children.

---

[23] Gil, David, *Beyond the Jungle*, pp. 15-17.

So when we're going home, we're in our own space. If someone violates that space, we get upset."[24]

The roads, however, are not the only places where increasing rage is being felt. As a walker, I know that people on sidewalks can be just as angry. In fact, wherever one goes in public, it seems people are not only getting meaner and meaner, but are becoming more studied and skilled in their ability to put each other down. There is a feeling of increasing anarchy in public spaces today. It feels more and more like one can do anything one wants since the guiding authority is "every man/woman for himself/herself."

The reason we behave so abysmally to each other is not just because less than 5% of the public owns more than 80% of the country's wealth,[25] it's because we don't know who we are. (If we did know who we are, that statistic would surely be leveled out.) The very concept of "finding yourself" is joked about in our culture as something only for the wealthy or loony or lazy or lost when it is really for the desperate—those who are so unsatisfied with the choices they see around them that they will do anything for authenticity. The rest of us are acting like we think we are supposed to be acting. We are taking on personas which have nothing to do with who we are or what we want. We see some persona we think we like and we claim it as our own. That's because we've lost our connection to reality.

There have been societies throughout history which have acted as counterpoints to our capitalistic "march of progress," societies which have been egalitarian, environmentally aware, spiritually in tune and so on. No one is saying that Native Americans were nonviolent, but they do stand out as an example of a kind of society that could teach us a lot

---

[24] Taylor, Michael, *Road Rage: Ugly Increase in Acts of Freeway Fury*, San Francisco Chronicle, June 16, 1997.

[25] Gil, David, *Beyond the Jungle*, p. 116.

about a spiritual connection to nature and to each other. Other examples would be many tribes in pre-colonial Africa, and even in Europe before the invasion of Western civilization. Of course, all of these people have been pretty much decimated by the "stronger" Western ideas of feudalism and capitalism and the idea that "might makes right." But one thing we can learn from these indigenous societies right now is their spiritual connection to life. This is something even capitalism cannot suppress once people learn of it.

I think that a change in consciousness is the only way we are going to change our paradigm from capitalism to something as liberating as capitalism was 500 years ago when it started to emerge out of feudalism. Of course, this change in consciousness has already begun. It began with the women's movement. It began with the environmental movement. It began with the civil rights movement in this country. It began with the gay liberation movement worldwide. To my mind, being a child of the '60s, it began in the '60s.

In fact the '60s is a really good place to look to see what works and what doesn't work in an "idealistic" or "utopian" society. Communes work when people are mature enough to govern themselves and not have to rely on some charismatic leader to inspire them. They don't work when people are strung out on drugs and just going along with the '60s mentality in the same way that young people go along with the times today—that is, by imitation.

One of the great exciting political upheavals today is the continuing movement towards democracy in the Middle East called the Arab Spring, which followed similar democratic uprisings in Russia, Eastern Europe and even China at the end of the Cold War in the last century. These are very exciting events and may be precursors to the eventual democratization of the economy in this country and worldwide.

Whatever happens will have the power of inevitability, and it will happen of its own accord because enough people will have raised their consciousness enough to be able to try something which is based on the premise that people are trustworthy. And to the people who have raised their consciousness, other people *will* be trustworthy.

The trouble with socialism is that we've all seen how terribly it worked out in Eastern Europe and the former Soviet Union. The innate laziness which capitalists always speak about really happened in those former Communist countries. Ironically, only when the Soviet Union was *competing* with the West did it excel, for example, in the race for space and with its Olympian athletes. But what if we had democratic socialism? Marx and Engels really thought political and violent, if necessary, revolutions were to be the only way that a classless society could be created.

What if, through education, we created a truly classless society? If, through education, we achieved a totally literate society in this country, would that create a revolution? If everyone was literate enough so that they could not only read but could get a glimpse of who they are (through their reading), then at least one aspect of who we are—our social class—would be greatly equalized. Would an educated class, as the United States (and the world, for that matter) is increasingly becoming, put up with CEOs making hundreds of times what the average worker makes and still call it "free enterprise?" Are CEOs really worth it? Maybe twice as much as the average worker. Maybe three times. But 100 times? 200 times? 300 times? I saw a bumper sticker recently that said, "Nobody gets a second home until everybody gets a first one." That doesn't seem unreasonable to me.

It will be the excesses of the capitalistic "shadow" of democracy which will be its undoing. And only through education can we see the full extent of that shadow and what it is doing to ourselves and our society. I am speaking of an education of body, mind and spirit. It is only when the spirit is connected that the body and mind can function at their optimum. Of course, our society is wary of speaking about spirit and education in the same breath. But unless a student's spirit is "turned on" by learning, they won't learn much. They will be soul dead, and they will stop learning. And they will forget whatever they have learned because they will not have connected to the vital center of their being. They will seek elsewhere in gangs or fraternities or sororities or corporate America to fill their empty souls, but it won't work because gangs and fraternities and sororities and corporate America have no soul to give them. Whatever soul is found in these institutions comes from outside the institutions, unless they are renegade corporations like Ben & Jerry's which tries to incorporate the socially conscious lessons of the '60s into the corporate world of profits.

We need to learn how to learn. Humanity's natural way to learn something is through induction, that is, by seeing how some particular thing works and then generalizing about all things. This works well in some instances. For example, by learning that a flame can burn my finger if I touch it, I can learn never to hold my hand over an open flame. However, if I apply the same method of inductive reasoning to categorize all people of a certain race or sex, then I have severely damaged my educational process.

Buckminster Fuller called this the disease of "categoryitis." It's the way we learn how to learn, but it can lead us into some deadly traps. Categoryitis can lead down the primrose lane of specialization. I am a botanist. I am an English teacher. I am a boy. I am a girl. I am black. I am white. Specialization forces us into individual paths of existence, cutting us off from each other and from ourselves. Extinction is what occurs if specialization is allowed to take over our lives. If an animal became such a specialist that it could only survive on one type of diet, for example, and if by some act of nature that diet were eliminated, that animal would become extinct.

Fuller sees the computer as forcing humanity out of its specialization by being such a super-specialist that it will force humanity to fulfill its natural function of being generalists. My own teacher, Thane Walker of The Prosperos, said of computers, that, if nothing else, they will show humanity how mechanical we are. By computing things better and faster than we can, computers will therefore leave us only ourselves. As my friend Michael Kelly says, there is a difference between computing and thinking.

Humanity's intellect is its greatest evolutionary tool and yet it is not the be-all and end-all of the Universe. Fuller estimated that during the last third of a century before the year 2001, that "the number of boo-boo's, biased blunders, short-sighted misjudgments, opinionated self-deceits of humanity will total, at minimum, six hundred trillion errors. Clearly, man will have backed into his future while evolution, operating as inexorably as fertilized ovaries gestate in the womb, will have brought about his success in ways as synergistically unforeseeable to us today as were the . . . developments of the last 150 years unforeseen by our wisest great-grandfathers of 1810. All of this does not add up to say that man is stupidly ignorant and does not deserve to prosper. It adds up to the realization that in the design of universal evolution man was given an enormous safety factor as an economic cushion, within which to learn by trial and error to dare to use his most sensitively intuited intellectual conceptioning and greatest vision in joining forces with all of humanity to advance into the future in full accreditation of the individual human intellect's most powerfully loving conceptions of the potential functioning of man in universe."

Fuller goes on: "To begin our position-fixing aboard our Spaceship Earth we must first acknowledge that the abundance of immediately consumable, obviously desirable or utterly essential resources have been sufficient until now to allow us to carry on despite our ignorance. Being eventually exhaustible and spoilable, they have been adequate only up to this critical moment. This cushion-for-error of humanity's survival and growth up to now was apparently provided just as a bird inside of the egg is provided with liquid nutriment to develop it to a certain point. But then by design the nutriment is exhausted at just the time when the chick is large enough to be able to locomote on its own legs. And so as the chick pecks at the shell seeking more nutriment it inadvertently breaks open the shell. Stepping forth from its initial sanctuary, the young bird must now forage on its own legs and wings to discover the next phase of its regenerative sustenance."

Fuller believes that we are "now" (he wrote this in 1969) at the point in our history of just stepping out of our just one-second-ago broken egg shell and that it is time for us to spread our wings and fly or perish.[26] We no longer can depend on the trial-and-error nutriment inside our egg. We are in a new relationship with the universe and need to think universally, as opposed to merely locally. It's time we become "Renaissance Men" again and give up some outdated and outmoded ideas. One of those ideas we need to give up, according to Fuller, is the idea of the Second Law of Thermodynamics, which states basically that everything in the universe is devolving and therefore whatever energy we spend must be spent carefully since there is only a limited amount. This is based on the solid state theory of the universe which was prevalent until only just recently. With the discovery of the speed of light at the beginning of the 19°' century, scientists discovered that stars that we see in the heavens

---

[26]   Fuller, Buckminster, *Operation Manual for Spaceship Earth*, p. 58.

may have long ago burned out. So we are seeing something that no longer exists. The universe is not a simultaneous event. It is a relative event.

The next idea we need to give up, according to Fuller, is Thomas Malthus' idea that humanity is increasing itself geometrically and the food supply is only increasing arithmetically. And then Charles Darwin came along and convinced the world that survival was only for the fittest. Marx, using this idea of the survival of the fittest, thought that the workers were the fittest since they were the ones who actually produced things, and so began the greatest political movement in the 20th century, Communism, which, along with its theoretical rival, capitalism, were both based on the assumption that there was not enough to go around.

Using the "law of the conservation of energy" which states that energy can neither be created or destroyed, Fuller concludes that "[t]he universe is a mammoth perpetual motion process. We then see that the part of our wealth which is physical energy is conserved. It cannot be exhausted, cannot be spent, which means exhausted. We realize that the word "spending" is now scientifically meaningless and is therefore obsolete." Therefore, since "the physical constituent of wealth—energy—cannot decrease and the metaphysical constituent—know-how—can only increase," Fuller concludes that "every time we use our wealth it increases . . . . When it is realized by society that wealth is as much everybody's as is the air and sunlight, it no longer will be rated as a personal handout . . ."

One more outmoded idea, by the way, which Fuller suggests we need to get rid of is the idea that humanity is naturally divided up into innately different races and nations which we hang onto with great pride. "Nations are products of many generations of local in-breeding in a myriad of remote human enclaves . . . which in the extreme northern hibernations bleached out the human skin and in the equatorial casting off of all clothing inbred darkly tanned pigmentation. All are the consequence only of unique local environment conditions and super inbreeding." Fuller also suggests that there is a tremendous crossbreeding going on in North America and especially in the Pacific Coast of North America where, he says, "a world type of humanity is taking the springboard into all of the hitherto hostile environments of universe into the ocean depths and into the sky and all around the Earth." Certainly Curiosity's recent trip to Mars is an example of that and I would add that not only are we diving into the hitherto hostile environments of the Earth and outer space but many of us on the Pacific Coast of North America are delving equally daringly into the inner reaches of the universe, into psychic research and so on in an attempt to redefine humanity itself as being more than mere automatons. We are helping to redefine humanity as being citizens of the universe.

Fuller says: "The procedure we are pursuing is that of true democracy. Semi-democracy accepts the dictatorship of a majority in establishing its arbitrary [i.e., based on "muscle, cunning, and weapons-established— sovereign-claimed lands and their subsequent legal re-deedings as 'legal' properties protected by the moral-or-no, weapons-enforced laws of the sovereign nations and their subsequent abstraction into limited liability-corporation equities printed on paper stocks and bonds"], ergo, unnatural, laws. True democracy discovers by patient experiment and unanimous acknowledgement what the laws of nature or universe may be for the physical support and metaphysical satisfaction of the human intellect's function in universe."

CHAPTER SIX

Equality

In *Democracy in America,* Alexis de Tocqueville's mammoth work, he says early on in his tome:

> Running through the pages of our history, there is hardly an important event in the last seven hundred years which has not turned out to be advantageous for equality.

> The Crusades and the English wars decimated the nobles and divided up their lands. Municipal institutions introduced democratic liberty into the heart of the feudal monarchy; the invention of firearms made villein and noble equal on the field of battle; printing offered equal resources to their minds; the post brought enlightenment to hovel and palace alike; Protestantism maintained that all men are equally able to find the path to heaven. America, once discovered, opened a thousand new roads to fortune and gave any obscure adventurer the chance of wealth and power.

> If, beginning at the eleventh century, one takes stock of what was happening in France at fifty-year intervals, one finds each time that a double revolution has taken place in the state of society. The noble has gone down in the social scale, and

the commoner gone up; as the one falls, the other rises. Each half century brings them closer, and soon they will touch.

And that is not something peculiar to France. Wherever one looks one finds the same revolution taking place throughout the Christian world.

I don't think de Tocqueville would be too surprised today at the revolutions that have taken place even in "un-Christian" parts of the world. Interestingly, even as long ago as 1830, de Tocqueville was talking about the inevitable emergency of two great world powers—the United States and Russia. America would succeed through taming its wilderness, he predicted, and Russia through taming its past. The latter could also be said about China while equality has always been the soul of America, slavery notwithstanding.

Much of the genius of de Tocqueville was his explanation of both the positive and negative aspects of having a nation whose soul demands equality. At what level are we all equal? Does equality discourage exceptionality? For de Tocqueville, the answer seemed to be a resounding "yes." He didn't think much of our literature or our leaders. For de Tocqueville, exceptional leaders or artists can only happen in exceptional times. During the Revolutionary War, exceptional times demanded exceptional leaders and thinkers. But in times of peace and plenty, our leadership tends to reflect the baser desires of the people. Democracy creates envy, de Tocqueville noted.

He compared entering the House of Representatives and finding obscure and vulgar men whose "people's representatives do not always know how to write correctly." In the Senate, however, "there is scarcely a man to be seen there whose name does not recall some recent claim to fame . . . . Every word uttered in this assembly would add luster to the greatest parliamentary debates in Europe." De Tocqueville's answer to the difference between the two houses is that in the Senate representatives were elected in two stages: first the people elected their own state legislatures and then the legislatures elected their Senators. In 1913, the law was changed to directly elect both Senators and Congresspersons. De Tocqueville would not have been pleased. Aristocratic governments, he thought tended to have better leaders even if they did tend to ignore the lower classes.

Confucius said: "When good government prevails in his State, he [the superior man] is to be found in office. When bad government prevails, he can roll his principles up and keep them in his breast . . . . To see men of worth and not be able to raise them to office; to raise them to office and not be able to do so quickly,—this is treating them with disrespect. To see bad men and not be able to remove them; to remove them, but not to send them far away,—this is weakness. If good men were to govern a country a hundred years, they would be able to transform the violently bad, and dispense with capital punishments."

In democracy as we know it today in the United States of America, there is the dictatorship of the common—common people, common ideas, common talent, common food. MacDonald's and Burger King do not thrive and flourish in a vacuum. They provide common food for common people. We may talk a good line about our love of entrepreneurship and of Mom & Pop restaurants, but a MacDonald's is just around the corner where Mom & Pop used to have their restaurant. And, in fact, Mom & Pop are probably at McDonald's right now anyhow.

Charlene Spretnak in *The Resurgence of the Real,* says, "Antitrust legislation finally broke up monopoly cartels in the United States at the beginning of this century, but today's core corporations have absorbed or knocked out so much of their previous competition that they exercise the very same control over a market as did the old cartels. The mega-retailers—Wal-Mart, Kmart, Toys "R" Us, Home Depot, Circuit City [sic], and others—play their suppliers against one another and abruptly shift their sourcing to countries with the cheapest labor. Just as millions of independent retailers have been pushed out of business, so have eight of the ten million farms that existed in 1950 in the United States. The permanent elimination of jobs now haunting the global economy was first experienced in the industrialized countries—always in the name of efficiency, economic growth, and modernization. In an economy that is owned by a relative few, economic growth benefits those few, not society at large."

Instead of buying into the idea of the "inevitability of the global marketplace," Ms. Spretnak suggests that we relearn the art of community-based economics. "The premise [of community-based economics] is simply that keeping money circulating largely within a city or region yields greater stability and security than having capital continuously sent out of the area to distant corporate headquarters. One of the reasons poor neighborhoods remain poor is that a very high percent age of money earned goes out of the community at the very first retail transaction. Community-based economics adopts several elements from the only long-term model of successful sustainability that we know: nature. Principal among these is the adaptability and security that results from diversity. Encouraging a wide range of economic activity in a town is a safer bet than trying to attract a TNC factory by promising tax breaks, spending millions of public dollars on extending the municipal infrastructure to the new plant, and then hoping that operations are not abruptly moved to a country with cheaper labor."

In order to reawaken our love for community, we need to reawaken ourselves from the slumber of the technology-induced trance which tells us that we live in a "global village." What kind of a village is it in which we see, but can't be seen, in which we know what is going on, but in which we are not known. No wonder people want to be famous. They want to be part of the global village instead of just another damn onlooker. What good is living in a global village if you are alienated from your next door neighbor? Or, put another way, if it does indeed take a village to raise a child, what happens when that village which raises your child is the Global Village?

It was not always this way. Ms. Spretnak, speaking of de Tocqueville, says: "De Tocqueville noted during his 1828 tour of the United States that we were singular as a citizenry in our propensity for forming clubs and organizations in order to address perceived needs in our communities. Until recent decades, most Americans came of age and lived out their lives in a rich social matrix shaped by communal pleasures and responsibilities. The historic accomplishment of the American political experiment was not only our well-balanced and resilient Constitution but also our grassroots solutions to the traditional Western tension between the individual and society: The structures of society were located not only in a government or even in the 'mediating institutions,' such as churches and labor unions, but also in a plethora of self-organizing groups, clubs, and associations. Quilting bees, hobby clubs, barbershop quartets, Chautauqua events, and youth groups of all sorts provided a weave of relationships that nourished American democracy. Government may have been somewhat distant, but the commonweal was not. 'Society,' structured with countless cooperative efforts, was no longer construed as an entity that is agonistic to the individual; rather, it made a richly relational life possible."

In 1830, de Tocqueville wrote: "In America the majority has enclosed thought within a formidable fence. A writer is free inside that area, but woe to the man who goes beyond it. Not that he stands in fear . . . , but he must face all kinds of unpleasantness and everyday persecution. A career in politics is closed to him, for he has offended the only power that holds the keys. He is denied everything, including renown. Before he goes into print, he believes he has supporters; but he feels that he has them no more once he stands revealed to all, for those who condemn him express their views loudly, while those who think as he does, but without his courage, retreat into silence as if ashamed of having told the truth."

De Tocqueville gave a special place to newspapers in the American democracy. He saw them as the very cradles of civilization—as a way for people to associate with each other through the ideas expressed in the newspapers and "the feebler [people] are individually, the easier it is to sweep them along." Reporters used to in fact be common people. Now they are highly paid and highly educated professionals. Of course, the public is a lot more educated than it was 100 years ago as well. But education, in itself, does not guarantee someone (whether reader or writer) who knows how to think for him or herself. Most of what we call thinking is simply mental computation anyway, unless one is truly an Individual in Wilde's sense of the term.

De Tocqueville pointed out that for a society to function it requires some ideas which everyone (or almost everyone) holds in common. In America, our prime motivating idea is the idea of equality. We began as a nation with the assumption that "all men [sic] are created equal." What this really means is that no one has a preordained right to rule over others as is true in despotism. Despotism tries to keep power by keeping walls up between the people. Equality puts people side by side with no walls, but no common links to hold them together either, such as loyalty to a king or even one's tribe. When one adds freedom to equality, then you have the beginning of a democracy in which people begin to understand the need for each other.

In America, work is respected while leisure is not. That's because, de Tocqueville points out,[27] work represents democracy and the working class while leisure represents aristocracy and the ruling class. Although there are servants in America, there is no servant class as there was in Europe at the time of his writing. And even though there are workers in America today, in a sense, there is no working class. For one of the prime ideas of America is equality. The workplace seems to be an unfortunate and (perhaps) temporary anomaly—something we have to put up with until "our ship comes in" or we win the lottery, or we find out what we truly want to do with our lives or until society shifts paradigms. Twenty years ago when I was reading books like Alvin Toffler's *Megatrends,* I was counting the days until I would have so much leisure I wouldn't know what to do with it all. Now I'm retired and still don't have time for all the things I want to do.

Industry tends to make workers' lives narrower and less rewarding financially and personally while management gets richer and richer by having invested in products which are being made better and cheaper. But management does not wish to rule workers as in traditional aristocracies—just to use them. There is no association between management and worker other than at the workplace. There is no noblesse oblige. "In any event," says de Tocqueville, "the friends of democracy should keep their eyes anxiously fixed in that direction. For if ever again permanent inequality of conditions and aristocracy make their way into the world, it will have been by that door [the door of management] that they entered."

---

[27] De Toqueville, *Democracy in America*, p. 550

CHAPTER SEVEN

Future Paradigms of Democracy

Dissatisfaction with modernism is certainly not new to our age. In the 19th century, Thomas Carlyle in *Past and Present* said "all work is noble." He appealed to the "Captains of Industry":

> The Leaders of Industry, if Industry is ever to be led, are virtually the Captains of the World; if there be no nobleness in them, there will never be an Aristocracy more. But let the Captains of Industry consider: once again, are they born of other clay than the old Captains of Slaughter; doomed for ever to be not Chivalry, but a mere gold-plated *Doggery* . . . ? Captains of Industry are the true Fighters, henceforth recognizable as the only true ones: Fighters against Chaos, Necessity and the Devils . . . ; and lead on Mankind in that great, and alone true, and universal warfare; the stars in the courses fighting for them, and all Heaven and all Earth saying audibly, Well done! Let the Captains of Industry retire into their own hearts, and ask solemnly. If there is nothing but vulturous hunger for fine wines, valet reputation and gilt carriages, discoverable there? Of hearts made by the Almighty God I will not believe such a thing. Deep-hidden under wretchedest god-forgetting Cants, Epicurisms, Dead-Sea Apsirns; forgotten as under foullest fat Lethe mud and weeds, there is yet, in all hearts born into this

God's-World, a spark of the Godlike slumbering. Awake, O nightmare sleepers; awake, arise, or be forever fallen! This is not playhouse poetry; it is sober fact. Our England, our world cannot live as it is. It will connect itself with a God again, or go down with nameless throes and fire-consummation to the Devils. Thou who feelest aught of such a Godlike stirring in thee, any faintest intimation of it as through heavy-laden dreams, follow *it,* I conjure thee. Arise, save thyself, be one of those that save thy country.

This was written in 1845 when there were one and a half million unemployed out of a population of 18 million in Eng land.[28] Carlyle believed or at least hoped for a new England in which "[t]o be a noble Master, among noble Workers, will again be the first ambition with some few; to be a rich Master only the second." "Liberty?" asks Carlyle rhetorically. "The true liberty of a man, you would say, consisted in his finding out, or being forced to find out, the right path, and to walk thereon. To learn, or to be taught, what work he actually was able for; and then by permission, persuasion, and even compulsion, to set about doing of the same! . . . [I]f liberty be not that, I for one have small care about liberty. You do not allow a palpable madman to leap over precipices; you violate his liberty, you that are wise; and keep him, were it in strait-waistcoats, away from the precipices! Every stupid, every cowardly and foolish man is but a less palpable madman: his true liberty were that a wiser man, that any and every wiser man, could, by brass collars, or in whatever milder or sharper way, lay hold of him when he was going wrong, and order and compel him to go a litter righter."

---

[28] *The Norton Anthology of English Literature,* Sixth Edition, Vol. 2, p. 965

From the viewpoint of the "noble Worker," Carlyle says: "The smallest item of human Slavery is the oppression of man by his Mock-Superiors; the palpablest, but I say at bottom the smallest. Let him shake off such oppression, trample it indignantly under his feet; I blame him not, I pity and commend him. But oppression by your Mock-Superiors well shaken off, the grand problem yet remains to solve: That of finding government by your Real-Superiors!"

We have such a worship of democracy and equality in this country that Carlyle's statement to "[find] the government by your Real-Superiors" smacks of blasphemy. And yet Confucius would understand with his idea of the "superior man." So perhaps would Nietzsche with his idea of a "superman" or Heard with his idea of the second maturity man or Richard Bucke. Richard Maurice Bucke in his book *Cosmic Consciousness,* speaks of "cosmic conscious man." He says: ". . . [J]ust as, long ago, self consciousness appeared in the best specimens of our ancestral race in the prime of life, and gradually became more and more universal and appeared in the individual at an earlier and earlier age, until, as we see now, it has become almost universal and appears at the average of about three years—so will Cosmic Consciousness become more and more universal and appear earlier in the individual life until the race at large will possess this faculty. The same race and not the same; for a Cosmic Conscious race will not be the race which exists to-day, any more than the present race of men is the same race which existed prior to the evolution of self consciousness. The simple truth is, that there has lived on the earth, 'appearing at intervals,' for thousands of years among ordinary men, the first faint beginnings of another race; walking the earth and breathing the air with us, but at the same time walking another earth and breathing another air of which we know little or nothing, but which is, all the same, our spiritual life, as its absence would be our spiritual death. This new race is in the act of being born from us, and in the near future it will occupy and possess the earth." Talk about a new paradigm!

Bucke expands in his book on several case histories of people he thinks have attained this new paradigm of consciousness. Among them were Buddha, Christ, Paul, Dante, Edward Carpenter, Walt Whitman, William Blake, Mohammed, Francis Bacon, Balzac and Plotinus. Cosmic Consciousness is defined as the next step up from self-consciousness. It is, in my mind, equivalent to Gerald Heard's second maturity—realizing that we have access to the "mind" of the universe and the sometimes frightening correlate to that idea: that the universal mind has access to us.

By believing that there are no "Real-Superiors," we are believing, by extension, that there is no Superior Mind, no mind superior to the human intellect, that there is no God. This is the ultimate modernist ideal—that man needs nothing outside of himself and his Scientific Method. This includes Nature. The modernist era believed in a rational, scientific, objective and therefore detached answer to the problems of mankind.

Postmodernism as a response to modernism falls into two categories: deconstructionists and ecological postmodernism (a term coined by Charlene Spretnak). Deconstructionists believe that anyone's reality is merely a social construct. Ecological postmodernism believes that we live in a dynamic relationship to the universe which includes God and Nature and that each of us is at the center of that universe; in fact, that each of us is at the fulcrum point between God and Nature. This is indigenous spirituality in the sense that we are all indigenous people as Universal citizens. We all belong here and wherever we find ourselves is sacred land. But this sense of the importance of place is certainly something we can learn from so-called indigenous people.

One of the basic premises of modernity is "progress," which sounds innocent enough except that modernists are often so concerned with a future progress, that they rarely have time to live in the present. And since there is no time other than the present, that makes them (us) a pretty disconnected group of people. Being connected to the present means being connected to one's body, one's spirit, and one's community as well as being connected to the totality of the universe. Perhaps the reason there are so many homeless in the streets of our cities is because there are so many of us who are spiritually homeless due to our false reliance on modernist goals which allow for no sense of place (belonging) or time. There is only a sense of the future when things will be unbelievably better and we'll be out of debt!

This makes ecological postmodernists a very spiritual bunch. When one realizes one's connection to everything, one realizes that everything has meaning. Things are not "merely" coincidental. They are *profoundly* coincidental. Jung uses the term *synchronicity* to express a moment of realization of the connectedness of all things. An ecological postmodernist realizes that the universe has a mind of its own that is even greater than the human intellect! And this Mind, if you will, is everywhere in Nature which includes us.

Thoreau believed that the very birds flying through the sky are a message to be read,[29] and so do I. We are reaching towards the "inevitable" global village through our multinational corporations and our multinational mentality. Loren Eisley in *The Unexpected Universe* says: "To [use a] biological analogy, it is as though, instead of many adaptive organisms, a single gigantic animal embodied the only organic future of the world." Octavia Paz says: "What sets world in motion is the interplay of differences, their attractions and repulsions. Life is plurality, death is uniformity. By suppressing differences and peculiarities, by eliminating different civilizations and cultures, progress weakens life and

---

[29]   Eiseley, Loren, *The Unexpected Universe*, p. 145.

favors death. The ideal of a single civilization for everyone, implicit in the cult of progress and technique, impoverishes and mutilates us. Every view of the world that becomes extinct, every culture that disappears, diminishes a possibility of life."[30]

Ben Cohen and Jerry Greenfield (better known as "Ben & Jerry") in their book *Ben & Jerry's Double-Dip* state that "[b]usiness is the most powerful force in society. Social problems cannot be solved without business in a leadership role."[31] If we are ever going to change society and thereby each of our lives, the world of business is the heart of the beast we need to tame. And there are many companies, what Ben & Jerry call values-led companies, which are doing just that: Patagonia, Inc. (clothing); Odwalla, Inc. (juice); Tom's of Maine, Inc. (personal care products); Blue Fish Clothing; Frontier Cooperative Herbs; Working Assets Funding Service [now called Credo] (credit cards and long distance phone service); Rhino Entertainment (music); Tommy Boy (music); Whole Foods Market; Just Desserts; Stonyfield Farm Yogurt; Aveda Corporation (personal care products) and more.[32]

These are all companies which are trying to live by their values in four different categories: (1) The quality of their work life (what it's like to work there). At Whole Foods Market, for example, grocery teams must approve or disapprove new hires by a $2/3^{rds}$ vote after usually a 30 day trial period. (2) Business practices. Are their business practices beneficial or harmful to the community? (3) The environment. How does the business effect the environment? Do they use recycled products or do they dump their waste in the local storm drain? (4) Social mission projects. On top of everything else, how do they contribute the society's needs? What

---

30 Highwater, Jamake, *The Primal Mind: Vision and Reality in Indian America,* Harper Collins Publishers, New York, NY 1981.
31 Cohen, Ben and Jerry Greenfield, *Ben & Jerry's Double-Dip*, p. 33.
32 Cohen, Ben and Jerry Greenfield, *Ben & Jerry's Double-Dip*, p. 47.

percentage of their profits do they reinvest in the community to help solve some of the problems of the community?

Work, for me, has always been my learning place. It is where I have, time after time, had to encounter my shadow self in the form of the dysfunctionality of my family coming to life over and over again in the people I work with. But I believe in therapy. I believe in the messages of my dreams and the birds flying overhead. And I believe that by paying careful attention to the details of my life, I can turn the dysfunctions of my workplace life into fulfilling work which will benefit both me and society.

19th Century English writer William Morris said of his age: "I hold that the condition of competition between man and man is bestial only, and that of association human . . . . A mask is worn by competitive commerce, with its respectable prim order, its talk of peace and the blessings of intercommunication of countries and the like; and all the while its whole energy, its whole organized precision is employed in one thing, the wrenching of the means of living from others. I tell you it is not wealth which our civilization has created, but riches, with its necessary companion poverty; for riches cannot exist without poverty, or in other words slavery . . . . What have you done with Lancashire? . . . Were not the brown moors and the meadows, the clear streams and the sunny skies, wealth? [Civilization] has let one wrong and tyranny grow and swell into this, that a few have no work to do, and are therefore unhappy, the many have degrading work to do, and are therefore unhappy [and their work alternating with "inevitable" unemployment and] the danger of periodical semistarvation."[33]

---

[33]   Thompson, Paul, *The Work of William Morris*, p. 234, quoting *The Collected Works of William Morris,* 24 volumes, London 1910-1915, edited by May Morris.

Morris also called the Victorian model of family "an affectionate and moral tiger to whom all is prey a few yards from the sanctity of the domestic hearth" and says, "There is the closest of relations between the prostitution of the body in the streets and of the body in the workshops . . . . If a professional man . . . does little more than his due daily grind—dear me, the fuss his friends make of him! How they are always urging him not to overdo it, and to consider his precious health, and the necessity of rest and so forth! And you know the very same persons, if they found some artisan in their employment looking towards a holiday, how sourly they would treat his longings for *rest,* how they would call him (perhaps not to his face) sot and sluggard and the like. [There were, of course, individual employers on good terms with their men] and really unconscious of the war between them . . . for the workman's real master is not his immediate employer but his *class,* which will not allow even the best intentioned employer to treat his men otherwise than as profit-grinding machines. "[34]

William Morris wrote *News from Nowhere* regarding a future society of communism and machinelessness due in great part to his love of and respect for Medieval life. He saw a future in which work was a central pleasure of life. "Nations, as political entities, would cease to exist; civilization would mean the federalization of a variety of communities great and small."[35] There would be no property and there would be equality of pay for *all* work. He felt that "[t]he aim [of progress] should be varied, pleasant, and as far as possible creative work for all, even if the only means was a simpler way of living. He was confident that with a lighter burden of work, a high standard of food and housing, and a

---

[34] Ibid, p. 245.

[35] Ibid, p. 253 quoting William Morris in *Commonweal*, 22 June1889; *The Letters of William Morris to his Family and Friends*, London 1950, p. 287.

general opportunity for education, all human beings were capable of a far higher development of their physical health and intelligence; capable of a responsibility, creative imagination and sensitivity sufficient for full democracy and equality."[36]

Morris was a mentor to John Ruskin who was part of the Arts & Crafts movement which sought to bring back craftsmanship in place of factory-produced items. Shakespeare, much earlier, was also a Medievalist. In his last play, *The Tempest,* Prospero, the magician king in the end gives up his magic and claims his rightful kingdom. Some see this as Shakespeare's way of saying farewell to the Medieval Ages and heralding the new modern scientific age.

Sir Francis Bacon shortly thereafter said, "by the agency of man a new aspect of things, a new universe, comes into view." Bacon was dreaming of the "new world of invention, of toleration, of escape from irrational custom."[37] In our rush into postmodernism, we mustn't forget the *toleration* that was an integral part of modernism when it was a new paradigm. Toleration was required for the new ideas which the scientific method was going to produce. Toleration also meant the end of a religious stranglehold on society. First came Protestantism, then came secularism, then came multiculturalism. Some say that we've taken toleration so far today, that people are hesitant to make any judgments at all. These supramodernists stand in a kind of impotent ascent to anything and therefore stand for nothing.

Coleridge, one of the leaders of the Romantic movement which stood as a kind of antithesis to the Enlightenment, talked about organicism as being based on a wholeness from within. Hierarchy, on the other hand, is based on the modernist ideas of the importance of parts. Nature was to be divided up to find out what makes Her tick. To the degree that we are

---

[36] Ibid, p. 255.
[37] Eiseley, Loren, *The Unexpected Universe*, p. 229.

part of a hierarchy in our family, work place or society, we are a part cut off from the whole. Perhaps the most graphic example of this in the 20th century was the Nazi Holocaust which was bureaucratic "reasoning" totally cut off from the heart. There was no compassion, no empathy, no guilt, even in those who were merely pursuing a scientific method to come to a "final solution."

To the degree that we live organically in the family, workplace or society, we can revolutionize our lives. It starts with each of us individually. By looking at our family history, we can reawaken the wholeness of each of us which inevitably was not fully recognized by our family or by ourselves. This will lead us to a work life which is fulfilling. We cannot have a fulfilling work life until we have sufficiently healed ourselves from our family life. And, finally, we cannot contribute anything to society until we have found a fulfilling work life.

I started out my civilian work life in 1968 under a boss named Chuck. I had the usual problems with authority figures which many young men have. It turned out, however, that all the time Chuck was acting as the supervisor (and the presumed superior) of our supply warehouse, he was taking supplies on the sly and selling them for his own profit. He was subsequently caught and prosecuted. Sometimes problems with authority figures are not just Oedipal in nature. But therein lies the rub. Figuring out which is which is the key to it all. Being able to act with righteous anger at a real abuse of authority instead of finding a likely person on whom to project one's youthful rage is the difference between being an adult and being a child.

A good example to me of organicism overcoming hierarchy took place at Princess Diana's funeral in 1997. At first Queen Elizabeth was going to simply stay away at her castle and mourn in private. But the public really demanded a stronger reaction from the Royal Family and finally got one. At the funeral itself, Diana's brother was applauded for the comments he made in support of his sister, but the applause came first from the people outside the church (the hierarchy) and was finally taken up by those in the church working from the back of the church to the very front. The final epitome of organicism overcoming hierarchy was symbolized when the Queen, who never bows to anybody, bowed her head to Diana's casket as it passed by her at the end of the service.

If organicism can overcome hierarchy in England's monarchy, perhaps there is hope for all of us everywhere.

EPILOGUE

As a direct result of the original writing of this paper in 1998 as my Master's thesis at the late, lamented New College of California, I came up with the idea of starting a nonprofit which we called "Buying With Vision." The nonprofit was to have given information to people on products and companies in regard to at least five different categories: 1) their effect on the environment; 2) the number of women and minorities in upper management; 3) what it's like to work there; 4) their social outreach programs; and 5) the healthfulness of the product itself. The project was a failure, but was, to me, in the best spirit of the Romantic movement of late 18th and early 19th century, in that action should follow education.

In September 2008, I retired from a 42 year work life and began a new career of volunteering. Shortly after the Occupy movement began in the United States on September 17, 2011, I joined forces with Occupy San Francisco and have been involved with them on an almost daily basis ever since.

They have become my democratic workplace.

BIBLIOGRAPHY

Bennett, Amanda, *The Death of the Organization Man,* William Morrow and Company, Inc., New York, NY (1990).

Bennis, W.G., *Changing Organizations,* McGraw Hill, New York, NY (1966).

Bennis, Warren, *Why Leaders Can't Lead: The Unconscious Conspiracy Continues,*

Jossey-Bass Publishers, San Francisco, CA (1990).

Berman, Morris, *The Reenchantment of the World,* Cornell University Press, Ithaca, New Yark (1981).

Bucke, Richard Maurice, *Cosmic Consciousness,* The Citadel Press, Secaucus, NJ (1973).

Cohen, Ben and Jerry Greenfield, *Ben & Jerry's Double-Dip: Lead With Your Values and Make Money, Too,* Simon & Schuster, New York, NY (1997)

Coles, Robert, *The Moral Intelligence of Children,* Random House, New York, NY (1997).

Confucius, *the Analects of Confucius,* Hartwick Humanities in Management Institute, Hartwick College, Oneonta, NY 13820.

Davis, Russell, *Freud's Concept of Passivity,* International Universities Press, Madison, CT(1993).

De Tocqueville, Alexis, *Democracy in America,* Harper Perennial, New York, NY (1969).

Eiseley, Loren, *The Unexpected Universe,* Harcourt, Brace & World, Inc., New York, NY (1969).

Fromm, Eric, *Escape from Freedom,* Holt, Rinehart and Winston, New York, NY (1941).

Fuller, Buckminster, *Operating Manual for Spaceship Earth,* Southern Illinois University Press, Carbondale, IL (1969).

Genesis, The Holy Bible, King James Version, Thomas Nelson & Sons, New York, NY.

Gil, David G., *Beyond the Jungle,* Schenkman Publishing Company, Cambridge, MA (1979).

Graebner, Norman A, *Freedom in America, A 200-Year Perspective,* The Pennsylvania State University Press, University Park, PA (1977).

Graves, Robert, *The Greek Myths,* Penguin Books, London, England (1960).

Heard, Gerald, Five Ages of Man, *The Julian Press, Inc., New York, New York (1963).*

Highwater, Jamake, *The Primal Mind: Vision and Reality in Indian America,* HarperCollins Publishers, New York, NY (1981).

Machiavelli, Niccolo, *The Prince,* Penguin Books USA, Inc., New York (1980, first published in 1532).

Marx, Karl, *Capital: A Critique of Political Economy,* Random House, Inc. Toronto, Canada (1906).

Marx, Karl and Engels, Friedrich, *The Communist Manifesto,* Washington Square Press, Inc., New York, NY (1964).

Miller, Alice, *For Your Own Good,* The Noonday Press, New York, New York (1990), 4th printing.

Mullahy, Patrick, *Oedipus: Myth and Complex,* Hermitage Press, Inc., New York, NY (1948).

Newberger, Eli H. and Richard Bourne, *Unhappy Families,* Clinical and Research Perspectives on Family Violence, PSG Publishing Company, Inc., Littleton, Massachusetts (1985).

Norton Anthology of English Literature, Volume II.

Pincus, Lily and Christopher Dare, *Secrets in the Family,* Pantheon Books, New York (1978).

Roche, Paul, *The Oedipus Plays of Sophocles,* New American Library, New York, NY (1958).

Rudnytsky, Peter L., *Freud and Oedipus,* Columbia University Press, New York, NY (1987).

Saunders, Tom M., Ph.D., *Go Ahead—Kill Yourself! Save Your Family the Trouble*, Distinctive Publishing Corporation, Plantation, Florida (1990).

Scarf, Maggie, *Intimate Worlds: Life Inside the Family,* Random House, New York, NY (1995).

Shorris, Early, *The Oppressed Middle: Politics of Middle Management, Scenes from Corporate Life,* Anchor Press/Doubleday, Garden City, NY (1981).

Smith, Huston, *The World's Religions,* Harper Collins Publishers, New York, NY (1991).

Smith, Tony, *Parzival's Brief case,* Chronicle Books, San Francisco (1993).

Spretnak, Charlene, *The Resurgence of the Real,* Addison-Wesley Publishing Company, Inc., Reading, MA (1997).

Tabin, Johanna Krout, *On the Way to Self: Ego and Early Oedipal Development,* Columbia University Press, New York, NY (1985).

Thompson, Michael, Richard Ellis and Aaron Wildavsky, *Cultural Theory,* Westview Press, Boulder, CO (1990).

Thompson, Paul, *The Work of William Morris,* The Viking Press, New York, NY (1967).

Thoreau, Henry David, *Walden,* New American Library, New York (1960).

Tzu, Sun, *The Art of War,* Oxford University Press, London (1963).

Whyte, *The Heart Aroused,* Doubleday, New York, NY (1994).

Wilber, Ken, *A Brief History of Everything,* Shambala Publications, Inc., Boston, MA (1996).

Wilde, Oscar, *The Works of Oscar Wilde,* P. F. Collier & Son Company, New York (1927).

Wiley, Ralph, *Why Black People Tend To Shout*, A Birch Lane Press Book, Carol Publishing Group, New York, New York (1991).

Zonta, Michael, *Adventures in Equality,* California Publishing Company, San Francisco, CA (1994).